IT ONLY HURTS
BETWEEN PAYDAYS

AMY ROSS MUMFORD

ACCENT BOOKS
Denver, Colorado

ACCENT BOOKS

A division of Accent Publications, Inc.
12100 West Sixth Avenue
P.O. Box 15337
Denver, Colorado 80215

Copyright © 1975, 1980, 1986 Accent Publications, Inc.
Printed in the United States of America

Library of Congress Catalog Card Number 75-17366

ISBN 0-916406-09-1

Thirteenth Printing

Dedication

This book is dedicated . . .

To the real "Mike" and "Lynn" for letting me share in the joy of their financial victory.

To both sets of parents who helped by *not* helping as Mike and Lynn learned to live by the bright red budget book; for their prayerful support—and for remaining my friends through it all.

To all young people, married or single, who are in financial trouble. My sincere prayer is that they will find something in this book to start them on the road to recovery.

To young couples about to be married. May they be challenged to set up their bright red budget book right from the beginning and avoid the pitfalls of financial mismanagement.

Appreciation

My Sincere Thanks . . .

To two friends and pastors, Dr. Earle E. Matteson and Dr. Hubert Verrill for their wise and helpful counsel.

To Haskal Gallimore and John Evans for providing valuable information and advice on the real estate chapter. And to Paul Riley and Darrell Baugh for their professional research and help with the chapter on insurance.

To my friend and co-worker, Violet T. Pearson, for patiently "listening" after each chapter was written, and for her expert editing of the completed manuscript.

And last, but not least, to my friend and boss, Dr. Robert L. Mosier for demanding my best and then trusting me to do it.

Amy Ross Mumford

Contents

The Problem With a Book Like This... 9

1/One Question—And I Was Involved 11

2/Ouch! The Sting of Reality 16

3/Is It a Tithe—Or Nothing? 24

4/Meet Your Bright Red Budget Book 33

5/Its Name Is Credit Card 47

6/Learning to Say, "I Can't Afford It" 53

7/Just Between You, Me and That Friendly Supermarket 60

8/Aiming at Goals One, Two and Three 69

9/The Unseen Dollars Behind Your Dream House 81

10/Looking for Alternatives Can Be Fun 91

11/An Intelligent Approach to Insurance 99

12/Planning for the Future 112

13/The Joy of a Bill Marked "Paid" 124

14/Cutting The Budget Pie Into Pieces 131

15/Who Promised You a Rose Garden? 140

16/Now That You're Finally Out of Debt! 146

"Let your manner of life be without covetousness, and be content with such things as ye have...."
                                        Hebrews 13:5

The Problem With A Book Like This...

Paychecks come in different amounts, colors, sizes and shapes. They vary from one job to another, from company "A" to company "B," and from one part of the country to another! For example: A recent survey, according to the 1984 Bureau of Economic Analysis report, listed the average annual per capita personal income for Alaska as $17,487. Mississippi was listed at $8,777. The national average was $12,789.

Houses are much the same. An $85,000 home in Denver, could sell for twice that amount in some sections of California. And an apartment in Washington D.C. could run three to four times higher than one in Omaha, Nebraska!

Interest rates change so fast it is impossible to settle on any given percentage and have it still accurate when the ink is dry on the next printing of this book.

That's the problem with a book like this!

The figures used in our examples probably won't match yours at all. But then, that's really okay. The real purpose of this book is not to see how closely we can come to your rent figure, your house payment, or your grocery bill. Rather it is to give you a plan, a set of principles to follow, that will help you gain control of your personal finances.

So, as we begin our trek from failure to success, keep your eye on the basics and follow the simple formula given. It will help you reach your goal. And to all the "Mikes" and "Lynns"—married or single—who are in financial trouble...

Happy Finances,

Amy Ross Mumford
Denver, Colorado

1/One Question—and I Was Involved

Mike and Lynn were two terrific young people with a shaky five-year marriage, a three-year-old son—and problems. All kinds of problems. One of which was the inability to manage their personal finances. Now, projecting sales, cost analysis, controlling inventory and keeping an eye on department budgets is a way of life for me. I'm in the habit of solving problems every day. Hearing Mike describe his financial dilemma created a reflex action in me.

I didn't set out to get involved. It just happened as the result of one well-meaning question. I didn't even take time to think about how it would change my life for the next several months.

I just said, "Mike, would you like some help organizing your finances?"

That's all it took.

With a catch in his voice, this heartbroken young six-footer quietly said, "I could sure use some."

Afraid he might change his mind, I asked, "When can we get together?"

"How about tomorrow evening?" he replied.

This was the beginning of a togetherness you may find hard to believe.

Mike's parents have been close friends of mine for many years, and Lynn's folks are friends of more recent days. I have been "Aunt Amy" to three-year-old Bobby since he was a baby. We were all concerned about Mike and Lynn. For several months the tension between them had been evident. The closeness—the oneness—was gone.

Being aware of this, we were still not prepared for Mike's phone call asking his folks if he could move back home—just until he and Lynn could reach a decision regarding their future. Lynn and little Bobby would continue living in their apartment.

Mike was like one of my own, and I was sharing the shock of this news with both families. Having just read that 75 percent of all broken marriages could be traced to money problems, I decided to stick my neck out—or my nose in.

This conversation between Mike and me took place in my car as we drove along a country road toward a cheery, sunny restaurant on the outskirts of town. We were on our way to meet his parents and young son for Sunday dinner.

He and Lynn had been separated for one short, agonizing week. His initial anger was exhausted. All that remained was the deep hurt and a feeling of failure and defeat.

When we arrived at the restaurant, Bobby flung himself into his daddy's arms—and held on. He was not too young to know that something was not right with his little world.

During dinner we all made a sterling effort to match the mood of our surroundings. The cheery atmosphere seemed to mock us. We talked all around the one question uppermost in our thoughts: "Was this young family, so dear to us, headed for divorce?"

As we walked to the parking lot, I asked Mike to bring every scrap of information he might have regarding their finances with him the following evening. Little did I realize what I was asking for, but the Lord knew and graciously led each step of the way in the months to come.

Driving home alone, along that country road, I began to think about Mike, Lynn—and money. Could this really be at the bottom of their separation, or was it a symptom of a more basic problem? Were 75 percent of all divorces actually due to disagreements over the dollar? Or, could money mismanagement just be the tangible evidence of an intangible weakness in the marriage structure?

Any young couple with opposing purposes in life, an inability to communicate, and a failure to exercise self-discipline in their personal finances is headed for trouble. If they separate, money problems are easy to blame.

On the other hand, a young couple with a common goal who can discuss their problems, and who know how to control their personal finances, can face the most devastating money crisis—together—and come out on top.

When the almighty dollar causes problems in

your marriage, you can fight and run—or you can stand together and fight your way out. It is your choice. Young married couples, however, do not have a corner on financial problems.

Single young people, whether away from home for the first time, or for a long time, can face many of the same problems. Single parents who have to make it alone also know the burden of trying to stretch that paycheck. In fact, runaway finances can happen at any age. At times, we all experience a lack of self-discipline when it comes to spending money. And the unexpected expense or disaster can catch anyone unawares.

The occasional setback or dose of overspending can be corrected, but Mike and Lynn's problems went far beyond this. They were *overcome* by their bills!

When Mike and Lynn saw a balanced budget replacing the maze of their indebtedness, they began to talk about the need for a book that would give practical help and a simple budget plan to young couples just starting out. And, of course, to those who are already in financial trouble. Mike felt that if he had been introduced to this simple budget plan before he and Lynn were married, they would never have lost control in the money department.

They encouraged me to tell their story and set forth the plan we used in working out their problems—not all of them past-due bills!

We will leave their story at times to cover subjects they felt should be included such as: how to look at tithing during a financial crisis; how credit cards

14

should be used; goal setting as a way of life; costs to be considered when buying a house; how to control the grocery budget; an intelligent approach to life insurance; how to plan for the future; and a look at percentage budgeting.

Let me be the first to admit that this is not a highly technical or sophisticated budget plan. But it is not aimed at solving the problems of highly technical or sophisticated budgets. It isn't geared to the fiscal policies of large corporations. It is geared to the financial plight of young people (and some not-so-young people), married or single with aching checkbooks and sagging spirits.

Also, this book is not written for those who are in control of their personal finances and have a good working system. It is written for "beginners" who are just starting out and need to learn to live within the limits of their income. It is also for those who have no budget plan, who need help and encouragement in getting organized and gaining control of their finances. Built into this easy-to-use system is the fun and self-satisfaction of watching your progress from one payday to the next.

The real "Mike" and "Lynn" join me in prayer that God will use our experience to bless and enrich the lives of countless others with a need similar to theirs.

2/Ouch! The Sting of Reality

Mike and I sat facing each other across my dining room table that first Monday evening—and between us lay that ominous pile of bills. I think we both wanted to run. And sometimes it is easier to run from reality than it is to face it, but running from a problem never solves it.

"Where do we begin?" Mike wanted to know. There was a note of discouragement in his voice.

Determined to be optimistic, I gave him a cheery smile and replied, "Just give me the facts."

If you have more bills than you can pay, this is the place to begin. Face the facts. All of them. Start with a blank piece of paper and at the top list your take-home pay for each payday in the month, and any other income you might have. These are the assets with which you have to work.

Next, list under liabilities everything you owe. There should be nothing left uncovered at this point. Expose every financial commitment you have.

That's precisely what Mike and I did. First, his assets—money to use. Second, his liabilities—for starters that pile of monthly statements on the table! Once we had them opened and sorted, we ended up with one car payment; a monthly insurance premium; seven past-due charge accounts, and a list of doctor bills that looked like the first page in "Who's Who in the AMA."

By now it was too late to run. I was hooked. This was going to be as much of a challenge to me as an over-sized bone is to an under-sized dog.

"Mike," I said, "It is pretty bad. Are you sure you want me involved in this?"

"Sure," he gulped. "I can't do it alone."

Even Mike and I, together, couldn't do it. But, we both knew Someone who could give us the wisdom and the strength to gain control of this situation. Two verses of Scripture came to mind: "I can do all things through Christ, who strengtheneth me" (Philippians 4:13) and, "If any of you lack wisdom, let him ask of God, who giveth to all men liberally, and upbraideth not; and it shall be given him" (James 1:5). We stopped and asked the Lord to do just that—give us strength and wisdom. We were going to need both.

It would have been great if all of Mike's take-home pay could have been applied to those past-due bills, but the usual monthly living expenses had to be added to the list. There was rent on the apartment, utilities, telephone bill, gasoline for the car, grocery money for Lynn and Bobby, and some spending money for Mike. Married or single, your list will not be too different.

After you have completed your list of debts and

monthly living expenses, you have a glimpse of reality, but don't stop there. That isn't the basic problem. You need to look the reason for your financial dilemma straight in the eye. Even if you live alone, and don't have a friend sitting across the table going over your past-due bills with you, you need to face your problem—whatever it is. It may not even be your fault, but before you can get on top of it, you have to know what it is.

"Mike," I asked, "what do you think has gotten your finances into this condition?"

After a few attempts to skirt the issue, he admitted, "Just charging faster than we could pay, I guess."

It was out in the open. We both started to laugh, for it was a rather obvious conclusion. Then, I did something I would never have dared do if I had given it that famous "second thought."

"Would you like me to take possession of your charge cards for the duration?"

To my amazement he said, "Fine," and before I could apologize for being so presumptuous, he was dealing charge cards out of his billfold as if that were the brightest idea he had heard all evening.

"Wow! You went too far," you are probably saying about now.

It *was* an extreme measure, but the Lord was leading, for it proved to be an excellent budget balancer. If you, like Mike and Lynn, have been charging faster than you can pay, there is only one way to correct the problem. Stop charging! And start paying. It is as simple as that. Call a moratorium on buying—until you have paid for everything you have charged.

Perhaps you can resist the urge to add to those convenient charge accounts. I hope you can. But, when the pressure is really on, it might help if someone else were in possession of *your* charge cards. Be sure it is someone you can trust. Or, better yet, you can take your scissors and cut them up! The credit card companies will be happy to issue you new ones when your accounts are current.

The reason behind your shortage of funds may not be charge accounts. It may just be installment buying. A middle-aged couple I knew was making four major installment payments a month. They had a new roof on top of the house, new carpeting inside the house, new furniture in the bedroom and a new Cadillac in the driveway! And, they were trying to keep up with several very active charge accounts at the same time. The pressure was too much. The end result—they sold their home, paid the bills and got a divorce.

You may even find that without charge accounts and installment payments, your money runs through your fingers like water. You have nothing in particular to show for it. It just seems to disappear.

This "money-through-the-fingers" problem often starts when young people first begin to work while still living at home. They are not faced with the full responsibility of maintaining a home. And, even if they are paying "board and room," it is probably a token payment. I know one single girl, living at home, who collects birds—ceramic birds, brass birds, glass birds, china birds—any kind of bird. She pays very little for the privilege of living at home, yet seldom has enough money to carry her through from one payday to the next. She is a prime candidate for the compulsive charge card club.

Whatever the reason behind your problem, it is important to think it through, recognize it for what it is, and face the problem straight on. Then, and only then, will you be ready to find a solution.

And a solution is what Mike and I were trying to find. When we finished writing down every financial responsibility he had, we came up with the following list.

(The figures used are the actual amounts of Mike and Lynn's original debts and their real living expenses. Your living expenses, monthly and yearly, will be much different.)

CHARGE ACCOUNTS
```
    Department Store #1 ................$480.
    Department Store #2 ................ 413.
    Department Store #3 ................ 200.
    Oil Company #1 .................... 440.
    Oil Company #2 .................... 200.
    Master Card ...................... 350.
    Visa ............................. 700.
         Total ...................... $2,783
```

MONTHLY EXPENSES
```
    Rent ................................ $175
    Utilities ........................... 35
```

Telephone........................... 9
Groceries........................... 200
Gasoline 80
Insurance 15
Car Payment 150
    Total.......................... $664

YEARLY EXPENSES
Car License .... $ 60
Car Insurance 180
Income Tax Service................. 40
    Total.......................... $280

MEDICAL EXPENSES
Doctor Bills....................... $1,000

Mike's finances were definitely in control of him! It would be exciting to reverse the situation and put *him* in control of them. From the look on Mike's face, however, he was not sharing my anticipation. Somehow, that look of defeat, discouragement and doubt had to be turned into something better.

"All right," I said, "let's begin to organize this mess."

Mike replied, "This I've got to see!"

When your initial list is complete, you are ready to divide it up and build a payment schedule. I prefer the twice-monthly budget plan, using the 1st and 15th of each month as the budget dates. The dates are not as important as the "schedule." Mike and Lynn obviously had not been following any sort of financial schedule, or plan. And, their story could have been completely different if they had worked out a financial plan before they were married, instead of waiting until after they were up to their ears in debt.

If you are in the same condition, you probably have not had one either. If you are a working single, living at home, the best thing you can do for your future is to set up a budget, no matter how simple, and learn to manage your finances. It's also a perfect time to begin a regular savings program.

If you are planning on getting married, don't wait until you are in trouble to think about a budget. Sit down together before the wedding and build a budget for your anticipated living expenses, and any debts you will be bringing into the marriage. Be sure to include a savings plan for the future.

This bit of counsel may be too late for you. If it is, follow along with Mike and gain control of *your* personal pile of bills.

We were ready to begin a rough draft of Mike's proposed payment schedule. He wrote, "December 1st," at the top of a clean sheet of paper, and added, "December 15th," about halfway down.

"Let's make your giving to the Lord the first item under both dates," I suggested.

Mike hesitated. "Wel-l-l, we haven't been able to tithe, so we haven't been giving anything to the church," he admitted. "But, I sure would like to."

Mike's remark opened up a subject that needed careful handling. Before we discussed how much he should give, I needed time to pray, study and talk it over with wiser heads than mine. Mike didn't need to be confused at this late hour. And besides, the sting of all this reality was enough for one night.

We decided to meet again on Friday—the day before his next payday. We would build his budget and pay his first schedule of bills.

3/Is It a Tithe—Or Nothing?

Trying to find the right guidance for Mike before Friday night started me thinking. Why do people tithe? I decided to find out.

One teenager I interviewed was experiencing some expensive problems with her car. Her somewhat angry reaction was, "I've been tithing! I thought God was supposed to keep things like this from happening!"

This is not too different from the adult who said, "I'm afraid not to tithe. I know that if I don't, something terrible and expensive will happen."

Tithing in these two cases falls into the category of buying "accident insurance," or is it "health insurance?" There is little joy in this kind of giving.

Next, I ran into a financially-wise, money-minded tither. "I figure I might as well give it to the church as to the government." To him it is an excellent tax deduction.

Then, there was the good-guy-with-the-white-hat tither. "I try to do what's right . . . and I give to the church." He thinks his good deeds and giving are just the price of a one-way ticket to Heaven.

Sad? Yes, but I'm happy to report that these were in the minority. Let me tell you about an experience I had, several years ago, with my little mother who was 81 years old at the time. I believe she represents the majority of tithing Christians who give because they love the Lord. They feel it is their privilege and responsibility to give back to God a portion of what He has given to them.

Mother was almost blind and could no longer enjoy reading for herself. One day as I walked through the door of her apartment, she handed me some papers, along with her mail.

"What's this?" she wanted to know.

Glancing at the papers, I replied, "It's information about the Faith Promise program at your church."

"Yes, I know that, but isn't there something I'm supposed to fill out?"

She was right. There was a card on which she was to list the amount of her faith promise. Mother faithfully tithed her limited income, and when her monthly pension check arrived in the mail, this was always the first check she wanted me to write. She frequently reminded me, "This is my tithe. What I put in Sunday School is my offering to the Lord." I guess I just didn't expect her to do more.

We filled out the Faith Promise card. I suggested $3, but she said, "No, make it $5."

Mother was not tithing to keep trouble from her door. She had had more than her share. And at her age, income taxes were the least of her worries. She was too smart to think she could buy her way into Heaven. It just never occurred to her to hold back anything she had from the Lord.

Of all the people I talked to, the most heartbreaking were young Christians, some single and some married, who, like Mike and Lynn, found themselves floundering in the quicksand of financial mismanagement. And almost without exception, they admitted that since they couldn't tithe—they were not giving anything to their churches. This is the group of people I want most to help.

Now, any research on tithing, or giving to the Lord, would be grossly incomplete without going to God's Word to see what it reveals on the subject. I decided to approach it the same way. Why did people in Bible times tithe?

The first reference I could find to the tithe was in Genesis 14. During the battle between the four kings from the North and the five kings of the South, Lot ended up a prisoner of war. When Abram heard the news that his nephew was a P.O.W., he took 318 trained men and, gathering some friends along the way, set out to rescue Lot.

In a surprise night attack, Abram defeated the enemies and brought back all the goods that were taken from Sodom—and Lot, too! On his way home, Abram was met by the king of Sodom who came out to thank him for his deliverance. He also wanted to reward Abram by letting him keep all the goods he had retrieved.

But Abram said, "No, thanks."

Another king also met Abram. His name was Melchizedek and he was not only king of Salem, but a priest of "the most High God." He brought food and refreshment for Abram and the weary men with him.

And—he blessed Abram. Genesis 14:20 tells us that, "And he (Abram) gave him (Melchizedek) tithes of all."

There was no law that said Abram had to give a tithe to Melchizedek. He didn't do it to receive a blessing. He already had that. I think he recognized the superior position of this unusual priest/king and through him expressed his praise to God and gratitude for His blessing.

I turned over a few pages in my Bible to Genesis 28, and ran into Abraham's grandson, Jacob. He had just been blessed by his father, Isaac, and sent to the land of his uncle in search of a bride. He stopped along the way for a night's rest and while he slept, he had a dream. In the dream God spoke to Jacob and promised him some rather staggering blessings.

Jacob's reaction, upon waking, was a bit surprising. He started with a list of conditions for God. He said, "If God will be with me, and will keep me in this way that I go, and will give me bread to eat, and raiment to put on, so that I come again to my father's house in peace; then shall the Lord be my God."

He ended with this bargain: " . . . and of all that thou shalt give me I will surely give the tenth unto thee."

Jacob wanted all the good things in life—first! Then, he would give the tenth of all he had to the Lord. God did bless Jacob just as He had promised, but He also let him experience some real problems along the way. Are you beginning to notice a striking similarity between people today and those in the Bible?

When God gave the law to Moses, He included tithing as a part of Israel's worship and responsibility. In Numbers 18:25,26, the Lord instructed Moses regarding the tithe. The Levites were to take a tithe from the children of Israel as their inheritance from the Lord. They, in turn, were to offer "a tenth part of the tithe" in the form of a heave offering unto the Lord.

The children of Israel were required by law to tithe. They had no choice—or did they?

You only have to read Malachi 3 to discover that at least part of Israel had stopped tithing.

God asked, "Will a man rob God?"

When they replied, "How have we robbed thee?" God answered, "In tithes and offerings." Malachi 3:7 indicates that their lack of giving was a result of being away from God.

I can almost hear you murmur, "But Christians today are not under law. We are under grace." And, of course, you are right. In fact, we could put it another way. We are not under law—we are under love! What Israel tried to do in obedience to God's law, we should *want* to do because of Christ's love for us—and our love for Him. It was because of His love that He did what man was unable to do. In Matthew 5:17, Jesus said, "Think not that I am come to destroy the law...I am not come to destroy, but to fulfill."

The most important question we have to answer is, "Do we have a right *heart* relationship with the Lord Jesus Christ?" If we do, our giving will not be a problem.

There is little said about tithing in the New Testament. The first mention is in Matthew 23:23. Jesus is rebuking the scribes and Pharisees: "Woe unto you, scribes and Pharisees, hypocrites! For ye pay tithe of mint and anise and cummin, and have omitted the weightier matters of the law, [justice], mercy and faith: these ought ye to have done, and not to leave the other undone." Verse 28 wraps up their problem: "Even so ye also outwardly appear righteous unto men, but within ye are full of hypocrisy and iniquity."

We are not left to wonder, however, about the New Testament pattern of giving. In I Corinthians 16:2 we read, "Upon the first day of the week let every one of you lay by him in store as God hath prospered him." What can we learn from this portion of Scripture?

First, *we are to be regular in our giving.* "Upon the first day of the week..." or the Sunday after your payday whether it comes every week, every two weeks, or once a month. The key is consistent, regular giving.

29

Second, *every Christian is to give.* "Let every one of you . . . . " You are not excluded, even if you are in the middle of financial chaos.

Third, *the amount is to be in proportion to your prosperity,* " . . . as God hath prospered him."

So far, these are all physical exercises. You are to give, to do it in a systematic fashion, and to give according to your prosperity.

Paul gets down to the heart of giving in II Corinthians 8:7-12. He is writing about giving to help the poor in the church at Jerusalem. The church at Corinth had been a bit lackadaisical in doing their part. Here's what he wrote:

Therefore, as ye abound in every thing, in faith, and utterance, and knowledge, and in all diligence, and in your love to us, see that ye abound in this grace [giving] also. I speak not by commandment, but by occasion of the [earnestness] of others, and to prove the sincerity of your love. For ye know the grace of our Lord Jesus Christ, that, though he was rich, yet for your sakes he became poor, that ye through his poverty might be rich. And in this I give my advice; for this is expedient for you, who have begun before, not only to do but also to be [willing] a year ago. Now, therefore, perform the doing of it, that as there was a readiness to will, so there may be a performance also out of that which ye have. For if there be first a willing mind, it is accepted according to that which a man hath, and not according to that which he hath not.

Let's go over verse 12 again. It tells us that we are to have a "willing mind," and that if we do, " . . . it is accepted according to that which a man hath, and not according to that which he hath not." There it is. Giving is a grace. It should abound in our lives—out of a sincere love and a willing mind. This goes back to having the right heart relationship with our Lord. When that is as it should be, we will have a willing mind and we will give as much as we possibly can!

I would like to go back to Mike and Lynn, and other young people in the middle of a crisis, who feel they must give a tenth—or nothing. Prosperity was one thing Mike and Lynn did not have. But Mike did have a willing mind. He wanted to tithe, but until it was possible, we would meet the other standards. He would put his giving first. It would be regular. And it would be given with a right heart relationship to the Lord.

There are two kinds of financial crisis. First is the one over which you have absolutely no control. It is just not your fault! It might be due to the loss of a job; a serious illness, with the accompanying medical expenses; the death of a husband or wife; a fire; an accident. We could go on, but you get the idea.

Second is the kind of financial crisis that is self-inflicted. I recently heard of one young couple who falls into this category. Within six months, they had purchased a new home, a new car—and a new boat! Could it be that they were trying to keep up with the Grodonoviches?

If you are responsible for your financial problems, you have moved away from God's perfect will for your life. Somehow your priorities have gotten out of focus. Or it may have been poor judgment on your part that got you where you are. Ask God to forgive you and give you the strength and discipline needed to correct the situation. And, even if it isn't your fault, the formula for recovery is the same.

Follow along with Mike and Lynn. Take the steps necessary to regain control of your money and rebuild your Christian testimony in the business community.

With a willing heart give God the first part of your income. He doesn't expect you to give what you do not have, but He does expect you to prove the sincerity of your love by giving what you can.

The tithe is every Christian's responsibility before God. It is a discipline that will influence all of your financial commitments. Make it your goal!

4/Meet Your Bright Red Budget Book

It was Friday night, and promptly at 7:30 Mike rang the doorbell. He was smiling, but his eyes and his greeting revealed what was going on inside.

"Hi! Here comes your walking disaster area!"

I laughed and replied, "Come on in. We'll have to fix that."

As soon as he was inside, he perked up and, with his nose in the air, asked, "What's that I smell?"

I was glad for the aroma of those just-baked chocolate chip cookies!

Once again Mike and I faced each other across my dining room table. Picking up the bright red, three-ringed notebook purchased earlier in the week, I said, "Mike, meet your new budget book."

With mock respect, he nodded his head and responded, "Greetings! You realize that I am expecting a miracle out of you!"

Looking him straight in the eye, I said, "No, Mike, we are expecting a miracle out of YOU."

This budget book that we are introducing to you is practical and even fun, but it is an inanimate object

33

with no power to straighten out your money problems. It's all up to you. The book contains the plan, but you have to work it.

There are three things you will need to implement this simple plan for financial recovery:

First, if you do not already have one, you need a checking account. If you are married, it should be a joint account.

Second, you need a "bright red" budget book. The color, of course, is not important. Yours can be green, blue, or black if you prefer. I just happen to like red! We used a standard 9 x 7 inch, three-ring binder; 8½ x 5½ inch ruled ledger paper and two 9 x 6 inch manila envelopes punched to fit the notebook.

Third, you will need an instant, and consistent, dose of self-discipline.

If you are married, there is one more thing that is a must. You will need the complete cooperation of both husband and wife.

A conveniently located bank will help you with the first requirement, and your friendly stationery store will supply number two. You cannot, however, purchase the third or fourth necessity for any amount of money. You have to be so serious about your financial recovery that you will work very hard to achieve these.

I opened Mike's new budget book so he could see how it was going to work. The first page was headed, "Yearly Expenses." These are the once-a-year bills that sneak up on you and play havoc with your regular monthly payment schedule. By listing them in the front of your budget book, you will be able to plan for them ahead of time. They should be added to the payment schedule for the appropriate month. This eliminates those surprise attacks! Here is how Mike's page appeared:

					CK#	Amount				
		Car License								
		1/15				60 00				
		Income Tax Service				40 00				
		4/15								
		Car Insurance								
		5/12 to 11/12				90 00				
		11/12 to 5/12				90 00				

YEARLY EXPENSES

Mike had only three such items to consider: car license; income tax service, and car insurance. If you own a home there may be other items such as property taxes, homeowners insurance, et cetera. If you are single and do not have a house or a car, you may not have to consider any of these. How to have the money to pay these Yearly Expenses is covered in chapter eight.

On the second page I had some good news for Mike and decided to start with it.

"Mike, since you get paid every two weeks and we are setting your budget up on a twice monthly schedule, you will have two paychecks a year that will be free and clear."

As I expected, anything that was going to be free and clear sounded great to Mike!

If you are one of the fortunate people who get paid every week, or every two weeks, it is still wise to cope with your monthly bills and living expenses on definite dates. There is, however, something you need to watch. Just because there are three (or five) paydays within one month does not mean that one of them is extra. Deciding which paychecks you can consider free and clear, takes a little planning. Let me show you what I mean.

Page two in Mike's budget book was titled, "Payday/Budget Date Schedule." Starting with his first payday in the new year, we listed every other Saturday for the remainder of the year. Then, we matched "budget dates" to the nearest payday to discover where the extra checks would fall.

Here's how Mike's schedule came out:

PAYDAY/BUDGET DATE SCHEDULE

				Payday		Budget Date	
				1/11		1/15	
				1/25		2/1	
				2/8		2/15	
				2/22		3/1	
				3/8		3/15	
				3/22		4/1	
				4/5		4/15	
				4/19		free	
				5/3		5/1	
				5/17		5/15	
				5/31		6/1	
				6/14		6/15	
				6/28		7/1	
				7/12		7/15	
				7/26		8/1	
				8/9		8/15	
				8/23		9/1	
				9/6		9/15	
				9/20		10/1	
				10/4		free	
				10/18		10/15	
				11/1		11/1	
				11/15		11/15	
				11/29		12/1	
				12/13		12/15	
				12/27		1/1	

Notice that in each case the payday right after the "free" check falls three days behind the budget date. (See 5/3 and 10/18.) In the month of May it took two paydays to get the schedule back into step. In October, it only took one payday to recover the three days' loss.

Be careful to work the schedule clear through to the end of the year—and don't take the extra check too soon! This guarantees that on the 1st and the 15th you will have the money in your checking account to cover your budget. It also allows for advance planning as to how you want to spend—or save—that free-and-clear paycheck.

If you don't get paid every two weeks, don't despair. The basic principles in this book will still work for you. The important thing is what you do with your paycheck when you do get it!

Before we look at the next section in the budget book, we need to return to our work sheet and build a payment schedule. This takes a lot of erasing and juggling, so wait until it is "firmed-up" before putting it in your book.

Last Monday night, Mike had ended with a clean sheet of paper with "December 1st" and "December 15th" written on it. Since Mike was hoping to tithe, we listed this as the first item under both dates. Next, we listed the monthly living expenses. Some, like groceries and gasoline for the car, would appear every payday. It took careful planning to decide under which date the other payments would fall. The car payment had to be made early in the month, so it was placed under the "1st." This meant that the rent, also due on the 1st, would have to come out of the 15th paycheck and be held in the checking account for two weeks until it was due on the 1st. One paycheck would not handle both.

Some loan institutions will cooperate by changing your due date to accommodate your new schedule. However, if you are unable to arrange this, be very careful not to spend one cent of money that is committed for payment of a future bill.

Next, and using only the minimum amounts required, we tried to fit those seven charge account payments into this new budget. Mike whipped out his little calculator and added up the two schedules. You guessed it! There was no way that Mike's take-home pay would cover those bills. Is it any wonder their marriage was in trouble?

"What do we do now?" Mike looked horrified.

Let me emphasize that there were no luxuries—not even many of the necessities—included in this new budget. It was bare bones! To hold to it was going to take extreme personal discipline on the part of both Mike and Lynn. It was time to share my research on tithing.

We discussed what I found in the Old Testament, and what I discovered in the New Testament. When we finished, I said, "Mike, the Lord knows and understands the mess you are in. You have already asked His forgiveness for your part in creating this crisis. He will also honor you for trying to meet the demands of your creditors and rebuild a Christian testimony in the financial area of your life."

He looked a bit puzzled. "What are you suggesting?" he asked.

"At this early point in your financial recovery there are just not enough dollars to go around," I explained. "The amount of your giving will have to be adjusted to a lower amount."

Mike's heart was willing and God's Word said he was to give "in proportion to his prosperity." At this point, Mike didn't have any prosperity. We adjusted the tithe to one-third. We agreed this was temporary. As soon as any bill was paid off, his giving would increase.

You may be facing the same struggle. You, too, may want to tithe, but there is just no way! Can I challenge you to determine what you *can* give and make it the first item in your budget? You can give every payday, out of a willing mind and heart, and you can increase the amount as the Lord prospers you. Don't let it be a "tithe or nothing" decision.

With the amount of Mike's giving lowered we were able to fit a payment on each of the seven charge accounts into the budget. Now we were ready to tie down the schedule in Mike's new book.

This is the next step. Right after the first two pages (Yearly Expenses and Payday/Budget Date), place a colored divider labeled, "Payment Schedules." If you don't have the kind you get at the stationery store, make it out of construction paper cut one-fourth inch wider than your ledger paper. In this section you will list the payment schedules for the 1st and the 15th of every month in the current year.

Unless your list is extremely long, you can have both paydays for the month on one page.

Since Mike's future was so unsettled, we decided to do only one month at a time. He could add the pages for the rest of the year later.

It was time to pay bills!

The first check Mike wrote was made out to the church—his first step toward faithful, consistent giving. As each check was written, Mike placed a check mark beside the amount on the budget page. Each check was sealed in its envelope, ready to be mailed *after* Mike deposited his paycheck. Here is how his first completed schedule looked:

DECEMBER						
1st	Church	✓		1	5	00
	Car payment	✓	1	50	00	
✳	Groceries (Lynn-Bobby)		1	00	00	
✳	Gasoline			40	00	
	Insurance	✓		15	00	
✳	Mike (Spending money)			25	00	
	Visa	✓		37	00	
	Master Card	✓		11	00	
	Oil Company #1	✓		50	00	
	Oil Company #2	✓		15	00	
	Doctor #1	✓		5	00	
			4	70	00	
15th	Church			15	00	
	Rent		1	75	00	
	Groceries		1	00	00	
	Gasoline			40	00	
	Mike			25	00	
	Telephone			9	00	
	Utilities			35	00	
	Department Store #1			50	00	
	Department Store #2			20	00	
	Department Store #3			35	00	
	Doctor #2			10	00	
			5	14	00	

This system provides a very practical way of keeping track of your expenses and a visual method of knowing when something is not paid. Since no charge cards will be used, and no checks written between paydays, the three items with an asterisk (*) will require cash. Mike, for instance, will deposit all but $140 of his paycheck. This amount will have to cover groceries, gasoline and Mike's spending money until next payday.

This is where self-discipline enters the picture. Just in case some of these guidelines slipped right by you, let's recap them.

(1) Write *all* checks the night *before* payday.
(2) Make your check for the church the *first* one you write.
(3) Have the checks that are to be mailed ready to drop in the box the minute your deposit is in the bank—even if they are early. This won't hurt your credit rating! It also helps control the temptation to hold back on maybe "just one payment." Let's call it the "deposit your check and pay bills fast" theory!
(4) Write no more checks until next payday.

There is one more section in the budget book. The first is practical. This one is fun. The divider is labeled, "Record of Progress." Mike's first page in this part of the budget book is headed, "Record of Giving."

RECORD OF GIVING

Date		CK#	Paid	Total
12/1		101	1500	1500

He listed the date, check number and the amount of his first check made out to the church. As paydays roll around he will have the satisfaction of watching the total grow—and at the end of the year he will have accurate records for his income tax report.

Each of the next seven pages represents one of those past-due bills. The name of the charge account is at the top of the page. The starting balance is at the right. Each time a payment is made, the new finance charge will be added to the old balance. The current payment can then be deducted. Remember, finance charges are deductible on your income tax report. Here are Mike's first entries on his "Record of Progress" pages:

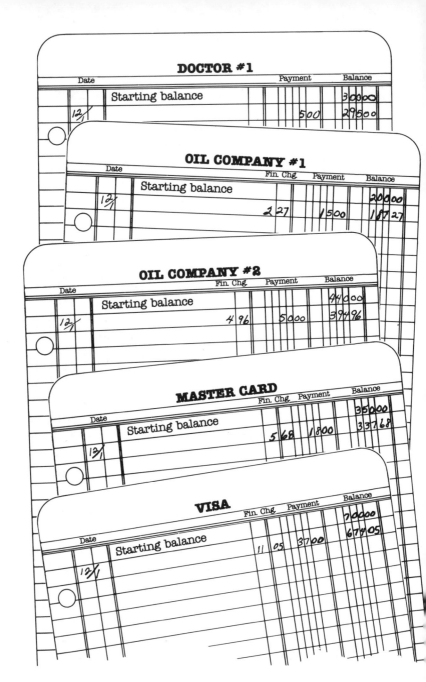

The challenge, and yes, the fun, of keeping this record of your own progress will soon have *you* hooked. You will be looking forward to next payday so you can deduct more payments and see those balances decline. Controlling your finances will soon become a way of life.

All that is left are those two manila envelopes, punched to fit your new budget book. Mark one the "1st" and the other, the "15th." Put them in the front, or the back, of your book. As your monthly statements arrive in the mail, place them in the proper envelope, along with other payment information needed. They won't get misplaced, and on payday, they will be ready and waiting!

Anything else you include in your personal budget book is limited only by your imagination. I'm a "record-keeper." I keep a list of charge card numbers; checking and savings account numbers; a complete list of Christmas gifts purchased from one year to the next; a record of all major purchases—and a graph of my weight. Whatever you add to yours, have fun!

When Mike had finished deducting his payments he looked up with a smile and declared, "This is going to be fun!" The look of discouragement, defeat and doubt was gone. Mike was still in debt— and he still had all of his other problems. But, now there was hope. He had a plan. He could see a light at the end of the tunnel. It wasn't going to be easy, but the unknown factor in his finances had disappeared.

We closed the bright red budget book with satisfaction and an impatient anticipation for next payday. We agreed to meet again in two weeks and tackle the payment schedule for the 15th. Before Mike left for home, we sat back and enjoyed tall glasses of cold milk and those just-baked cookies.

Yes, we were going to have fun—at least on paydays. In between, it was going to hurt for awhile!

5/Its Name Is Credit Card

After Mike left, I sat for awhile thinking back over the evening. I couldn't get those seven charge accounts out of my mind. The minimum monthly payments amounted to $225. And, of that amount, $44 went for finance charges.

How could two intelligent Christian young people get so involved in credit buying? And, yet, I knew they were not the exception to the rule. Too many of their friends were living the same way.

Were they unaware of God's principles regarding money? I picked up my Bible and started looking for familiar passages on this subject.

Matthew 6:24-34 covers it beautifully. This portion of Scripture starts out, "No man can serve two masters: for either he will hate the one, and love the other; or else he will hold to the one, and despise the other. Ye cannot serve God and [money]."

Verses 25-32 teach what the Christian's attitude should be toward the physical and material things in life. Look at verses 25 and 26: " . . . [Be not anxious] for your life, what ye shall eat, or what ye shall drink; nor yet for your body, what ye shall put on. Is not the life more than [food] and the body than raiment? Behold the fowls of the air; for they sow not, neither do they reap, nor gather into barns, yet your heavenly Father feedeth them. Are ye not much better than they?"

We are not to be concerned about *things*. They are not to sidetrack us from the more vital part of life. Verse 33 makes it plain. "But seek ye first the kingdom of God, and his righteousness, and all these things shall be added unto you."

It's a matter of priorities.

Could it be that the bombardment of advertising urging children, young people and adults to buy-buy-buy, is drowning out the sound of God's call to put Him first?

There is one television commercial that makes it sound so easy: "Our credit card will extend your income. Just buy what you want, when you want it. You can pay for it all at once—or a little at a time."

The product they are selling is a credit card. It is a small piece of plastic, approximately 3½ inches by 2 inches in size. It has been carefully designed to fit your billfold so you need never be without it. A highly computerized system has assigned it a number.

I just took a quick look at some of mine and they are even attractive. One is gold and white; another red, white and blue. Each one has my name pressed right into the plastic. Credit cards are personal—and very convenient.

If you are a member of the card-carrying class,

you can purchase all of your gasoline from your favorite oil company with a credit card. You don't even have to have one of theirs. They will take any one of the "major credit cards." You never have to be concerned about having cash when your tank runs dry.

You can even walk into a department store with only a few coins in your pocket and walk out a few minutes later with a new suit, dress, a set of pots and pans—or a china bird. All you have to do is present your plastic card and add your signature to the charge slip.

By now you are probably wondering if I am building a case against credit cards. I'm not. They are attractive, personal and convenient. But—they are just what their name implies. Cards which allow you to "buy now and pay later." And, pay later you must! By ANY name they are NOT another kind of money. The sooner you can look your credit card right in the eye and say, "You are *not* money!" the better off you will be.

While working with Mike, and in talking with other young people, I have discovered that they are victims of the times in which we live. They have been convinced that they can buy almost anything they want with a little plastic credit card. Many are charging themselves right into bankruptcy. Or—like Mike and Lynn—into the battle of their lives as they try to pay off the charges that were so easy to incur.

For credit cards to be helpful, they should be used—but never abused. If you can't pay the full amount when those monthly statements arrive, you are abusing them. Perhaps you are thinking, "Then, why do the stores list minimum payments on their statements if they expect me to pay the total due?"

The stores *don't* expect you to. Nor do they *want* you to. A major part of their profit depends on your doing just the opposite. One national chain of stores is reported to have said that they would have to go out of business if it were not for the profit gained from the interest on their charge accounts.

Think about this. If your charge account goes over 30 days, in some cases 90 days, the store where you made the purchase is actually *lending* you the money for the unpaid balance—with interest. And money lending is big business!

The "Truth-in-Lending Act," passed by the United States Congress in 1969, took the cloak of secrecy off the mysterious "finance charge." The lender, or charge account seller, must give you the actual annual percentage rate of interest, as well as the dollar amount of interest charged.

Take a look at the small print somewhere on your charge account statement. You will probably see something like this: "Monthly Periodic Rate 1.75 percent." This varies in different states, and it doesn't sound like much, does it? But read on.

The annual percentage rate will be listed as 21 percent. Compare this to other annual percentage rates in the lending market. An automobile loan may be as high as 13½ percent; a home mortgage loan, depending on the going rate, anywhere from

10 to 14 percent. An annual percentage rate of 21 percent on day-to-day purchases looks less and less like good money management.

Young people on their own, who may have their own credit card for the first time, are very vulnerable. There is a certain feeling of financial freedom that comes when that little piece of plastic is tucked inside your billfold! You no longer have to wait until payday to purchase something you want. You can eat out at that fancy restaurant even when you are broke. The urge to buy is no longer controlled by the availability of money in your pocket, or the balance in your checkbook. And that is the danger of credit cards. They make it tempting to live beyond your income.

There are several TV commercials beamed at young, single credit card holders. There is one in particular that shows an attractive young couple having dinner at an expensive restaurant. When the waiter brings the check, the young woman says, "Let me." She pulls out her new credit card and presents it to the waiter. It looks so sophisticated and easy. And, of course, the young man says, "I'll get it next time." But come the first of the month, her statement will arrive in the mail. Let's hope she can pay for it before the finance charges are added. If not, it could become a very expensive dinner.

If you were to ask, "Are you for, or against, credit cards?" I would have to reply, "It all depends."

Let's sum it up.

- Credit cards are personal and attractive.
- Credit cards are convenient.

- Credit cards are safer to carry than cash.
- They do *not* extend your income.
- They are *not* another kind of money.
- The interest charged is high.
- They can be properly used, or badly abused.

I am for credit cards when they are used within the limits of your monthly budget. I am against them when they become a reckless way of buying yourself into debt.

If you can afford a $50 a month payment on charge accounts, then limit your purchases to $50. Put that amount in your budget and stick to it. Don't, however, let yourself get into the habit of thinking you have to spend the $50 whether you need to or not.

I have to admit that when Mike and Lynn are out of debt, and once again take possession of their credit cards, I will be praying that they will have learned their lesson. It will all depend on whether or not they learn to say, "We can't afford it."

6/Learning to Say, "I Can't Afford It"

What a difference a date makes—especially when it is with your wife. With his head in the air, and a spring in his step, Mike bounded up the walk. As he handed me his coat, I noticed that this time his eyes were smiling.

As we automatically headed for the dining room, he said, "I took Lynn out for dinner last night—and we talked. We talked more than we have in months."

"I'm so glad, Mike," I said. "Tell me about it."

"Well, for one thing, we know that we want to get back together," he said with determination.

Then, he went on to explain.

"We both agreed, however, that we need some time to find out where we went wrong. We don't want to repeat the same mistakes."

I nodded my approval.

Rearranging his lanky frame in the chair, he added, "Lynn has already started counseling with the pastor. He wants her to come once a week, and as soon as he is ready for me, I will go with her."

More than Mike's finances were on the road to

recovery! A new, improved future for him and Lynn was beginning to take shape. It was the answer to many prayers.

Before we tackled the budget for this payday, Mike brought me up-to-date. Lynn had agreed to give up the apartment. The move was scheduled for Monday night. Mike's grandmother was going to store their furniture. Lynn and Bobby were going to stay with her parents, and Mike would continue living with his.

Mike opened the bright red budget book, laid his checkbook on the table and unzipped his pocket calculator. Then, as if he couldn't put it off any longer, he blurted out, "I overspent a little on that dinner last night."

"How much is a little?" I asked.

"Well—we didn't realize when we ordered that everything on the menu was a la carte. When the check came, it was over $30."

He made a real effort to make $30 sound like a "little."

The budget allowed Mike $25 spending money every two weeks. This had to cover his personal needs and an occasional day on the town with little Bobby. Spending $30 for one dinner meant that he had to write a check. In other words, he had to "rob Peter to pay Paul." This was the moment I had dreaded in this financial togetherness.

"You knew before you went that it was an expensive restaurant, didn't you?" I asked.

"Yes, but that was where Lynn wanted to go." He replied, defending himself. He quickly added,

"And, it was worth every penny of it."

I wanted to say, "Of course, it was worth it. Take her to the moon, if you can recapture what you have lost in your marriage." But, this was not the answer.

Another of Mike's basic problems was about to surface. It is the one that lurks behind practically every shattered budget. At sometime we are all guilty of it. It is the inability to say to ourselves, or anyone else, "I can't afford it."

Lynn was fully aware of their shortage of money. She had had a hand in creating the problem. She also knew how hard Mike was trying to get on top of it. She should have asked, "Can we afford it?" And, Mike should have felt free to reply, "No, we can't," and know she would understand.

When you want to do something, or buy something, which you know you cannot afford, there are two ways in which you can react. You will find them both mentioned in Hebrews 13:5: "Let your [manner of life] be without covetousness, and be content with such things as ye have . . . ."

The first part of this verse warns against living a life that is controlled by a desire for things. We usually think of covetousness as wanting something that belongs to another person, but it also covers the unrestrained desire for things you cannot afford. This way of life is filled with discontent—and indebtedness.

Jesus said in Mark 7:21-22, "For from within, out of the heart of men, proceed evil thoughts, adulteries, fornications, murders, thefts, covetousness, wickedness, deceit, lasciviousness, an evil eye, blasphemy, pride, foolishness." The sin of covetousness is listed right along with those we like to think of as the "big" sins.

The second part of the verse, " . . . and be content with such things as ye have," could well be engraved on the front of your budget book. This doesn't mean you are not to work to improve your financial status, nor to set goals for the things in life that you want. It simply means to be happy and at peace with yourself, today, as you live within your income.

In Philippians 4:4-7, Paul says, "Rejoice in the Lord always; and again I say rejoice. Let your moderation be known unto all men. The Lord is at hand. Be anxious for nothing, but in everything, by prayer and supplication with thanksgiving, let your requests be made known unto God. And the peace of God, which passeth all understanding, shall keep your hearts and minds through Christ Jesus."

In verse 11 of the same chapter, Paul states, " . . . I have learned, in whatever state I am, in this to be content." Even Paul had to *learn* to be content. And, if he could in the face of all of his troubles, you can, too!

I like the last part of verse 5. "The Lord is at hand." You don't have to learn this lesson alone. Bring your requests to Him. He will teach you contentment—and give you peace as a bonus.

Mike admitted that he had never been able to say, "I can't afford it." The result: seven past-due charge accounts and one $30 dinner, a more recent proof.

These four little words are equally as important to good money management as facing reality, building a payment schedule, or moving into a bright red budget book.

A serious Mike began paying bills, checking off each item as he went. Since there was no rent to pay this month, he had planned to have the extra $175 to apply on the charge accounts and doctor bills. With his $30 dinner, now there was only $145.

Lovable, impulsive, unpredictable and full of surprises—that's Mike. Tonight was no exception. We were about to discuss how best to use the $145, when he said, "Oh, by the way, here are a couple of bills that came this week."

The return addresses on the envelopes identified them as book clubs! I questioned Mike and learned that the books—and their bills—would keep coming on schedule until he canceled them. Then, he broke the news that he belonged, not to two, but to four book clubs!

Mike loved books! I was not too surprised.

"How did you ever get involved with four of these deals?" I asked.

"I don't really know," he answered, "I guess the offer always seemed too good to pass up."

This was a classic example of not saying, "I can't afford it." The timing was perfect.

If you are tempted to feel a bit smug and think, "I would never get mixed up with *four* book clubs," stop and think about it for a minute. You may not belong to even one book club, but if you have mismanaged your finances, look for *your* weak spot.

One young mother admitted that hers was falling for every special on baby photographs.

There's good news—and bad news—for the single person. The good is that there is no "Mike" or "Lynn" to throw your budget into a tailspin. On the other hand, you have no one to encourage you to say, "I can't afford it." No one to remind you that it's time to stop spending, signing up, or joining! You have to be *self*-disciplined. Remember the young woman who couldn't resist buying birds?

Mike agreed to cancel the book clubs. We paid the two bills and had $135 left.

When extra money appears in the budget, deciding where to use it is important. It may come from an extra job, overtime work, or even a cash gift. Don't just blow it. It is a great opportunity to get ahead of your schedule. And the sooner you have those past due bills paid off, the sooner you can begin your new life—one where you are in control of your finances.

Here's what to look for when you have extra money: the balance due and the size of the monthly payment. In Mike's budget, Visa had the largest balance, but the monthly payments were only $37. Department Store #1 was the second largest balance and the monthly payment required was $50. Since this would free the most dollars per month, we decided to add the $135 to the regular $50 payment in the budget. Mike turned to the "Record of Progress," and deducted the $185 payment from the balance due. This would be the first charge account to be eliminated.

As Mike closed the budget book, we both felt the strain of the evening.

"How about going over to the Ice Cream Shoppe and getting something just loaded with calories?" I asked.

Mike grinned, and with a twinkle in his eye replied, "I'd really like to, but I can't afford it."

"For a lesson well-learned, I'll treat!" I gladly responded—and off we went.

7/Just Between You, Me and That Friendly Supermarket

Over our hot fudge sundaes, piled high with whipped cream and sprinkled with nuts, Mike and I decided it was about time to include Lynn in our Friday night bill-sessions. Mike had a head start in learning how to manage their finances. She needed to catch up.

Lynn and I had had no contact since she and Mike had separated. I wasn't sure how she felt about my involvement in their personal finances, but if there was going to be any strain, I wanted it out of the way before our next meeting.

Early the next week, I picked up the phone, breathed a prayer, and dialed the number.

"Hello, Lynn? Could you have lunch with me tomorrow?"

"I'd love to." She replied, sounding pleased.

We met the next day at a lovely Mexican cafe in a nearby shopping center. It was good to see Lynn again.

As the gaily uniformed waitress walked away with our order, we smiled at each other. Lynn brought me up-to-date on little Bobby. Then, after a few minutes of the usual kind of chitchat, she opened the subject of finances.

"I appreciate what you are doing to help Mike get on top of his bills."

"*His* bills, Lynn?"

She winced. "I'm sorry," she said. "I guess they are *our* bills, aren't they?"

"That's right, Lynn," I gently replied. "I don't think either one of you could have gotten this deeply in debt all alone."

She nodded her agreement. This was the opening I needed.

"Do you understand the working arrangement Mike and I have regarding your finances?"

"I'm not sure," she replied.

"Let me explain. We have agreed to meet on the Friday before every payday. After all the bills have been paid for that part of the budget, no other check is to be written until we have first discussed it. If you were not one hundred percent in agreement with this, it could create some problems."

"What kind of problems?" she asked with a puzzled look on her face.

"For openers, you might begin to feel that how you and Mike spend your money is none of my business. And basically that's true. But, if that were to happen, I would no longer want to be involved. I can only help if I know what's going on."

"Mike doesn't seem to resent it," she said. "In fact, he's really excited about having a budget."

"I know," I smiled, "but, are you willing for the same kind of togetherness, the same control? Mike wants you to come with him a week from this Friday. Instead of the usual two-peas-in-a-pod, there would have to be three."

Lynn laughed and said, "Count me in as pea number three."

As quickly as the laugh came, it disappeared. Fighting to keep the tears back, she quietly said, "I just know we need all the help we can get."

Now our team was complete. All members were present, accounted for—and ready to go. A guarantee of success.

We spent the next few minutes catching up on the problems in their financial mismanagement. They boiled down to three:

(1) Charging faster than they could pay. They were both impulsive spenders.

(2) Trying to handle their finances without a schedule—no flight plan. Also known as "flying blind."

(3) Not being able to say, "We can't afford it." A real shortage of self-discipline.

Lynn was soaking it up like a blotter. She would be able to help Mike in many areas.

"Mike is going to work on that third problem this week, Lynn, and he is going to need your encouragement and full cooperation."

"Oh, I'll really try," she promised.

Changing the subject somewhat, I said, "Just between us, where do you think *you* need the most help in managing money?"

She groaned. "I guess my biggest problem was running out of grocery money before payday!"

Can you sympathize with Lynn? I can, but let's face it, those tempting, tantalizing items and displays at your friendly supermarket are out to get you! You have to enter the store with your guard up, or you will lose the battle before you reach "Aisle E."

If you are striving for a balanced budget and trying to learn good money management, it has to reach right into that grocery cart. The cost of food ranks right up there with rent and car payments. But it is also the one area where, with careful planning, *you* can have control. Short of moving, or selling your car, the other two are fixed amounts, and you can do nothing about them. But, you *can* stretch that grocery dollar from payday to payday.

The principles that follow work just as well for singles, single parent families, or couples of any age.

First you need to be creative—use your imagination. Once you get in the habit, you will come up with more and more ideas. Here are a few suggestions to get you started.

Take a look at your cupboard or pantry. Is it stocked with fad foods? Those munchy, crunchy snack foods you devour while watching TV? How about those expensive convenience foods? They may be time-savers, but only the busy rich can afford them. Erase such items from your grocery list.

"Ouch!" you say, "that is going to take the self-discipline you've been talking about."

You are right.

If you are not in the habit of working from a grocery list, here is one way to begin. Get out your favorite recipes, add a few new ones for variety, and plan your menus for the next two weeks, or for the number of days between your paydays.

Check the recipes you have selected and list the ingredients you do not already have. As soon as you can after payday, shop for everything on your list that can be stacked, stored, frozen, or refrigerated. Include the items needed for breakfasts and lunches. Estimate the amount of money you will need to purchase perishable items such as milk, fresh fruits and vegetables. Set this aside for use as needed. Don't carry this amount with you until you are ready to go to the store for that carton of milk!

"Whoa!" you shriek, "how do I know what I will feel like having for dinner that far ahead of time?"

You don't.

But, if you have carefully planned and shopped for that many meals, you can decide from one day to the next which one you want to fix. And, it will guarantee enough food to last until payday.

You won't run out!

"There's another way to watch your grocery budget, Lynn," I said. "Eliminate those wasteful leftovers."

With an exaggerated sigh, she said, "I watch them, but a lot of good it does. If I make a large meatloaf, planning to make it last for two meals, Mike keeps eating until there isn't enough for that second meal."

Laughing, I said, "There is even a way to control that."

This idea can be applied to many of your favorite recipes. You are limited only by your imagination. Instead of making one meatloaf, double your recipe, and make individual loaves. Set aside the number needed for one meal. Then, individually wrap and freeze the remainder for future use.

No leftovers!

This is especially helpful for people who live alone. You can have enough meatloaf for several meals—all ready to pop in the oven or microwave. And the smaller loaves take less time to bake. Here are some other ideas to start you thinking:

Spaghetti sauce with meat
    chili
      vegetable stew
       lasagna
        chicken dishes
         and more.

You can also make two pies and freeze one;
  a cake and freeze half,
    and part of that batch of cookies.

The list is endless.

You can set aside one day or evening a week and cook and bake several items to freeze. This is much less expensive than the frozen meals at your supermarket. And healthier, too!

You can't, of course, double every recipe the first two weeks, but you can begin to build a reserve as you go along. Are you beginning to see how this can stretch your grocery dollar, and also save you countless hours in food preparation?

To tie down all we had talked about, Lynn and I decided to make a list of "Guidelines for Grocery Shoppers."

Here it is:

(1) Plan menus for the number of days between paydays.
(2) Make a grocery list and stick to it.
(3) Do main shopping right after payday.
(4) Reserve amount of money needed for perishable items.
(5) Never shop for groceries when hungry.
(6) Avoid impulse purchases.
(7) Watch pricing. Store brands or generic items are often cheaper than national brands—and just as good.
(8) List price next to item and keep a running total as you shop.
(9) Don't be tempted! Avoid fad and snack foods.
(10) Watch for special sales on staple items.

Lynn's big brown eyes were shining and her words tumbled out. "I'm so excited. I can hardly wait for Mike and me to start keeping house again. I never dreamed there was so much to learn about grocery shopping—and cooking!"

You are probably asking yourself, "Does this mean I can never go to a restaurant for dinner?"

Of course not.

But if your finances are in as serious a condition as Mike and Lynn's, you will need to watch every cent you spend for awhile. However, as you begin to see the light at the end of the tunnel, or even before, you can plan a night out as a part of your food budget. (Hopefully, you won't spend $30 for two people until your bills are caught up!) There are fun, and inexpensive places to eat. It's up to you to find them.

Just remember, your food dollar is one of the largest items in your budget. It can be the most difficult to control. But it also offers the greatest opportunity for economy.

I asked a friend who is single and lives alone how she manages to stretch her food dollars. She said she saves coupons and watches for "double-coupon" days at the store. You may not have these in your area, but watch for the coupons that often come in the mail. Be sure to use only the ones for items you need and would be buying anyway. Don't be tempted to buy items you don't need just because they are less expensive with a coupon. She also watches for specials on staple items and stocks up on these. She limits her entertainment in her home to snacks or desserts rather than dinners. She said, "You can have a great time over a pan of warm brownies."

Whether you are single or married, you can protect your grocery budget by being a careful shopper. Can I challenge you to take a close look at the way your food allowance is being spent? You will be amazed at how wise planning can stretch that budgeted amount. Try it.

Lynn and I walked to the parking lot together. It had been a fun—and extended—lunch hour. But my mind was at ease about working with Lynn. I was looking forward to her coming with Mike for our future meetings.

Lynn's parting words were, "Just between us girls, I think Mike and I will have a much better life together after all we've been through."

I agreed.

8/Aiming at Goals One, Two and Three

The wind was whistling around the front door as I hurried to open it for Mike and Lynn. Hand-in-hand, they dashed into the house. They were both laughing. Shutting the door behind them, Mike breathlessly said, "Look what the wind blew in."

Taking her coat, I said, "Welcome, Lynn, we're glad to have you join us in the battle of the budget."

We headed for the dining room. Once again, Mike and I were on opposite sides of the table, but this time Lynn was close beside him. She seemed a little nervous.

Mike put his hand over hers on the table and said, "I know *I'm* happy she's here!"

That did it. She smiled at him, and then, sitting up straight, she looked at me as if to say, "Let's get started."

"Before we plunge into paying bills," I said, "there is something we need to discuss, okay?"

This was probably the first time they had ever sat down together to calmly discuss their finances, let alone pay bills. Starting right was so important.

Either one of them could defeat this effort. They had to realize the importance of working together as a team—with each one lending the other strength when the temptation came to buy what they couldn't afford.

"Lynn," I began, "Mike has been making real progress, whacking away at the mountain of bills you two managed to pile up. When you move into a new apartment, the budget will be even tighter. It is going to take every ounce of self-discipline you both can muster to hold the line until the last bill is paid."

Lynn moved a little closer to Mike and slipped her arm through his.

"I don't want to sound like a prophet of doom," I continued, "but if you do not learn to manage your personal finances efficiently, the two of you don't have a ghost of a chance of making your marriage work. You won't last one year!"

A very sober Mike said, "I believe it."

In marriage, it takes two to succeed. You cannot do it alone. If, while you are trying to gain control of runaway debts, your mate continues to charge and spend beyond your ability to pay—it just won't work. If the desire to balance the budget is one-sided, try to resolve it through an open, frank discussion. If this doesn't work, seek help and counsel from someone outside. A happy marriage depends on it.

Not realizing that I was touching a nerve, I added, "You need to agree right from the beginning that, if necessary, you will be each other's conscience. If one wants to buy something that you cannot afford, the other will have to remind the erring partner. And—that person must agree not to get mad when reminded!"

Lynn picked it right up. "It's like the other day. Mike wanted to buy something and I told him we couldn't afford it." She hesitated and went on. "Are you saying that he should accept the reminder and not get mad at me?"

Mike blushed and sheepishly grinned at me.

"Mike, you didn't!"

"I'm afraid I did," he confessed.

Lynn hastened to defend him. "If the roles had been reversed, I probably would have reacted the same way. It's just not what we are used to doing. We'll both have to work at it."

Satisfied that they understood the consequences of not learning to manage their money with complete cooperation, I moved our attention to the bright red budget book.

Mike proudly started at the beginning and showed Lynn how each section worked—from the "Yearly Expenses," right on through to the "Record of Progress." She eagerly took it all in and then asked, "When can we start paying bills?"

Laughing at her impatience, I said, "How about right now?"

For the next half-hour or so, they were lost in their world of "high finance." The characters! They were actually having fun paying bills.

When they finished, we decided to total the balances due on the seven charge accounts and see how much progress had been made. Picking up his little calculator, Mike started adding as Lynn read the balances out loud. We were amazed. The total due had been cut by a little over $500—in six short weeks! This led to the next subject on my list.

Goals!

Goals are the magic stimuli, or incentives, in life which incite you to do the impossible. A person without a goal ambles nonchalantly through life—accomplishing little. But, find the people who are making things happen and you will find goal-setters.

The Apostle Paul was no exception. In Philippians 3:13,14 we find his life goal. It's a good one for Mike and Lynn—and you—to follow:

"... *this one thing I do, forgetting those things which are behind, and reaching forth unto those things which are before, I press toward the mark for the prize of the high calling of God in Christ Jesus.*"

Paul was not dealing with our particular subject of finances, but there is an excellent principle here. Forget the past—a way of life displeasing to God. And, reach forth to the future and a life lived in the center of God's will. This is a spiritual goal and under its umbrella should come all of the physical and material goals in a Christian's life.

With this in mind, we are going to look at three very down-to-earth, practical goals. They are the *immediate*, the *short-term* and the *long-range*. It is important to work these out together. When you have them clearly defined, list them in the front of your book as a reminder to reach for them.

Goals are equally as important for singles and single parents as they are for couples. Your list may be somewhat different than Mike and Lynn's. That's okay. If you have a stack of past-due bills, hopefully, at least one will be the same. If you are single, your long-range goal may include a trip to Europe or some other distant land. If you are a single parent, one of your goals may be braces for Billy's teeth, or a trip to Disneyland with the kids. Goals are necessary if you want to measure progress and be able to look back and say, "This year I accomplished something worthwhile!"

There was no question about Mike and Lynn's *immediate goal.* It was to reunite their family. This would require one month's rent and the security or damage deposit on a new apartment.

We turned to the "Payday/Budget Date Schedule" in the front of their budget book to see how soon it could help them reach that goal.

Sure enough! There was one of those free and clear paychecks coming up. It wasn't going to be as soon as they had hoped, but we earmarked it for that purpose.

Without too much discussion, they agreed that their *short-term goal* was two-pronged. The elimination of those seven charge accounts—and the installation of the full tithe. To reach this goal and have it qualify as "short-term," would demand consistent payments every payday and patient adherence to the "no charge policy."

A *long-range goal* seems harder to reach simply because it takes longer. But, it is the kind that makes a dream come true. Your dream may be to own your own home, acquire more education, start your own business—or perhaps own a 40-foot yacht. Whatever it is, it will never happen until you *start* reaching for it.

Inspired by all of this goal setting, Mike said, "I know that before too long we want our own home."

There it was.

All three goals were clearly defined. Mike and Lynn could see how they were going to manage the first two, but the third was going to be a bit more difficult—or so they thought.

I had been waiting to introduce Mike and Lynn to a more positive side of personal finances—the automatic savings account. This was an ideal time.

"As soon as you have reached your short-term goals, I would like to get you started with two automatic savings accounts," I announced.

Mike's eyes opened wide. "*Two* savings accounts?"

I laughed at his reaction. They didn't even have one—and I was suggesting two.

Maybe you are asking the same question. I'll explain. The first one might be a regular Passbook

Account. The interest rates for these are low, usually 5.25 percent, but it is one way to get started with a small deposit. It is also an account where you can deposit and withdraw without any interest penalty. This first savings account has two purposes: Short-term goals and emergencies. Under short-term goals can fall the "Yearly Expenses." You can also finance your vacation and pay cash for larger items you would have charged previously.

While you are saving for what you want, or need, your money will be earning interest—and you will *not* be paying those finance charges. A double saving!

This account can act as a buffer fund to care for the emergencies that visit everyone from time to time. To be sure you are covered adequately, determine a minimum amount that you wish to leave in this account as the "emergency cushion." You may want to start with $100—$200 as a beginning, but try for $1,000 or more later. Then, what you save over and above this amount can be withdrawn for your short-term goals.

The second savings account is to start you on the way to the realization of your dream—your long-range goal. Nothing short of an earthquake should make you dip into this one. As soon as it reaches $500, you should visit your banker and have him explain the various investment options, with higher interst rates, that are open to you.

One option is the "time deposit," where you agree to leave the money in the bank for a specified period of time. The longer you agree to leave it, the higher the interest rate. You can plan the length of the deposit to coincide with your long-range goal. This gives you a certain incentive to leave the money in the bank. However, should you need the money before the time period has expired, you can withdraw it and take the interest penalty.

Now, let me try to sell you on the automatic savings plan. This simply means that you authorize the bank handling your checking account to transfer, once a month or every payday, a specific amount from your regular checking account to your savings account. If you get paid on the 1st and the 15th, you might have them take out one amount on the 1st for your regular savings account, and on the 15th another amount for your long-range account.

It pays to shop from one bank to another to see what kind of an account will be best for you and where you can get the best interest on your investment. You might want to look into a Money Market account where you have to maintain a certain balance to keep the higher rate of interest.

As soon as possible, it would be wise to have your first savings account transferred to this type. You can usually write up to three checks each month without a service charge. This is ideal for your short-range goals—and the minimum deposit then becomes your buffer fund. But, you will have to wait until you get the required amount to open such an account. This amount varies from bank to bank, so don't be afraid to ask.

The automatic method of saving is the secret to an account that grows—and grows. The amount should be listed in your regular monthly payment schedule as "Automatic Savings." The only difference between this and your rent is that you are paying *you*! Be sure to enter the amount in your checkbook just as if you had written the check. Even if you forget, you can be sure the bank won't, so treat it like any other bill that is due.

Another benefit of the automatic savings plan is that it completely does away with the need to make a decision on payday as to the amount you can "spare" for the savings account. If you are like me, you will not make it to the bank before it has been "needed" elsewhere.

Mike and Lynn were not ready to open one savings account, let alone two, but the idea was exciting. They added it to their list of other goals. For these we fixed a new page to go in the front of the bright red budget book. The title, of course, was "Goals." You can make your own list, but here is what Mike and Lynn's looked like:

GOALS

			Date	Reached
IMMEDIATE				
Rent for new apartment				
Security deposit				
SHORT-TERM				
Clear following debts:				
Master Card				
Visa				
Department Store #1				
Department Store #2				
Department Store #3				
Oil Company #1				
Oil Company #2				
Doctor Bills				
Install full tithe				
Automatic Savings #1				
Automatic Savings #2				
LONG-RANGE				
Buy house				

Perhaps you are thinking, "Why doesn't Mike get a second job and bring in more income?" Or, "Why doesn't Lynn go to work?" These, of course, are options to consider. Mike, however, worked nights and his schedule already limited their time together. Mike and Lynn were trying to rebuild a shaky marriage as well as gain control of their finances. Because of this, we decided it was far better for Lynn to be home with little Bobby and for them to have as much time together as possible. And, they needed to learn to live within their income at this time.

If you have been having problems with your finances, an extra job may be just the answer for you. If you are married, it might be wise to make it one where you can work together. Here are a few ideas:

(1) Find an office building that you can clean together in the evening.
(2) Work together in a fast food restaurant on Saturdays or some evenings.
(3) Consider getting an early morning paper route.

You may have other ideas. The important thing is not to let this extra job keep you apart. When you are recovering from battered finances, you need togetherness like never before in your lives.

Mike and Lynn left that night the same way they came—hand-in-hand. Their eyes were shining with the prospect of reaching that immediate goal. They were already making progress on the short-term goals—and they could at least begin to dream about the long-range goal.

Mike looked back over his shoulder as they started down the walk, and said, "Doing this together was sure better than doing it alone. Thanks!"

9/The Unseen Dollars Behind Your Dream House

Mike had been talking with one of the young men at work who was getting ready to buy a house with a VA loan—and no down payment. Mike was excited at the prospect and their long-range goal seemed to move closer—right up to the end of those seven charge accounts.

As we discussed this one evening, I asked, "Do you have any idea, Mike, what it costs to move into a new house?"

Mike was looking only at the price of the house, but that was just the beginning. There are some unseen dollars behind any dream house that must be considered. I decided to get some facts and figures and when the time came, help Mike and Lynn go into home ownership with their eyes open, aware of the different options, and with the tools to make wise decisions.

There is a fine Christian real estate agent in Denver named Haskal Gallimore. I shared with him my concern for young couples who jump into buying a "dream house" only to find out a few months later that it has turned into a nightmare.

And all because they were not aware of the total expenses involved in buying—and owning—a house.

Haskal agreed to help and then said, "In dealing with young couples, I try to find out if they can afford to buy the house in question. If I know they are getting in too deep, I advise against it."

There are no doubt others who feel the same way, but unfortunately, too many real estate salespeople are interested only in making the sale. And too many people, of all ages, get caught up in the excitement of buying a new house and fail to raise the questions that I hope we will put into your mind.

We decided to use specific examples to illustrate the choices that may be open to you when buying a house. For the first example, let's take a new house selling for $50,000. This is low, but it is a nice round figure to work with. And since Mike and Lynn would probably elect to go with a VA loan, we will, too. The same formula, however, can be used to analyze any mortgage proposal.

We'll assume it is a full (no down payment) VA loan, at 11 percent interest per year and that you plan to amortize it (pay it off) over 30 years. One of the first questions you need to ask is, "Can we afford the monthly payment?"

Four items need to be considered to arrive at the figure that will have to appear in your budget in place of rent. They are: principal, interest, taxes and insurance. The first two are referred to as "P & I," and all four as "P.I.T.I."

Here is the monthly payment breakdown on our first example:

```
Principal and interest .............. $476.16
Taxes (approximate) ..............    50.00
Insurance........................    13.00
   Total P.I.T.I....................$539.16
```

To qualify for this loan, Mike and Lynn would need approximately three and one-half times this amount, or $1,887 gross income per month. That is, *if* they have no other payments except for utilities. When the seven charge accounts and the car are paid off, they could move in. It would, however, be a foolish thing to do for it isn't really that simple.

Most new houses come equipped with carpets, a stove, hood with fan, garbage disposal and dishwasher. The buyer must provide the washer, dryer, refrigerator, drapes and landscaping. Here is where that number two savings account becomes important. In it you should have enough money to cover the following:

```
Closing costs........................ $1,000
Appliances.......................... 1,000
Drapes (minimum)................. 1,600
Landscaping (minimum) ........... 1,200
   Total .......................... $4,800
```

To finalize this deal as listed, you would need at least $5,000 set aside to pay for the initial expenses. If you were to sign on the dotted line—and didn't have it—can you picture the charges and install-ment payments that would once again appear in your budget?

Once you have decided to buy a house, don't rush into it. Wait until you have saved the money needed to do it right. And then, ask questions and get answers! Few lending agencies will *offer* this information. Here are a few choices open to you:

You can...
- buy a new house, or an older one
- apply for a VA (for veterans), an FHA, or a conventional loan
- choose to amortize it over 30 years, 25 years, or less
- make no down payment on VA loans
- pay as little as 5 percent down on others
- assume an existing loan

Most buyers prefer the traditional FHA or conventional loan with a 30 year fixed-rate mort-gage. There are other adjustable rate mortgages, but these are less popular.

If you are assuming an FHA or a VA loan, there will be no increase in interest rates. On other types of loans the rates can increase. In some states the maximum allowable increase is 1 percent. Check the law in your state before deciding.

Now, let's go back to your new $50,000 home, purchased with a VA loan and no down payment. Here's how to find out the amount of interest you will pay in 30 years.

```
P & I ($476.16) x 360 months  =  $171,418
         Less price of house         50,000
              Interest paid       $121,418
```

That's a bit of a shock, even if you were expecting it! Now, see what happens if you elect to make a down payment. With a VA loan this is called a "privilege." On this loan, for every $1,000 you pay down, you can deduct $9.52 from your monthly P & I payment.

We'll assume that you have $5,000, or 10 percent, to pay down. That would take $47.60 off of the $476.16 and bring the P & I payment down to $428.56. Follow this through:

```
$428.56 x 360 months  =  $154,281
     Add down payment          5,000
            Total paid     $159,281
     Less price of house        50,000
         Interest paid     $109,281
```

Without the down payment the interest paid was $121,418. You have just saved $12,137 as a result of the $5,000 down payment. But your financial know-how doesn't end there. Remember the $47.60 per month you have saved on the P & I payment? If you hadn't made the down payment, it would have had to be paid every month. And, *if* you were to put it in the bank, here's what it would amount to—not even counting interest.

$$\begin{aligned} \$47.60 \text{ x } 360 \text{ months} &= \$17,136 \\ \text{Plus interest saved} &\quad \underline{12,137} \\ \text{Total gained} &\quad \$29,273 \end{aligned}$$

And all because of that automatic savings account introduced earlier in this book!

Now let's see what happens if you decide to shorten the amortization period from 30 to 25 years, or 300 months. It will add $13.89 to your monthly P & I payment, bringing it up to $490.05. Add the taxes and insurance and your monthly P.I.T.I. payment would be $553.05. Your gross monthly income would have to be $1935.

$$\begin{aligned} \$490.05 \text{ x } 300 \text{ months} &= \$147,015 \\ \text{Less price of house} &\quad \underline{50,000} \\ \text{Interest paid} &\quad \$\ 97,015 \end{aligned}$$

A savings of $24,403! And all you had to invest was the additional $13.89 per month, or a total of $4,167. (This is without a down payment.)

If you choose to consider an older house, there are some advantages. It usually includes everything you would find in a new house, plus the drapes, refrigerator and fully developed landscaping. (You can often negotiate for the washer and dryer.) Here is the cash you need:

Closing costs........................$1,000
Washer and dryer................... 500
Total $1,500

However, there are also some disadvantages to

consider if you decide to buy an older house. You may be inheriting ten year old appliances, hot water heater and furnace. The carpet and drapes may be ready for replacement. You may find yourself facing expensive repairs within a few months. Check these out before signing any papers. Ask to see the bill of sale on any items in question.

In buying a house look for signs of water in the basement. This can be difficult to detect in a new house. A house may have to go through a very wet season before it shows up. Here are some things to watch for:

- A musty smell in the basement. If you notice one, ask about it.
- A white lime line close to the floor line. This, however, can be camouflaged with paint, wall paper or new baseboards.
- Two areas that are easily overlooked are the bottom of the furnace and under the staircase. Check these for water marks.

It is a good idea to check the ground and any concrete laid near the house. Be sure they slope away from the house for good drainage. Don't be shy about investigating every aspect of the house and yard. You may also want to check with the neighbors to see if they have had water problems. Any problems you don't foresee will be yours to solve.

Be cautious when considering a house "For Sale By Owner." If the facts about the condition of the house are misrepresented, you will have no re-course but to sue. When buying through a real estate company, you are protected by the law which makes the company liable for any claims they make regarding the house.

If the owner wants to carry the loan on the house you wish to buy, obtain the services of a good lawyer. Have him check the contract, the title and represent you at the closing.

Before you get discouraged with all of these facts and interest figures, there is something else you need to consider. If you were to continue renting at an average cost of $350 per month, here is what it would come to in 30 years:

$$\$350 \times 360 \text{ months} = \$126,000$$

The monthly payment in the first example given was $539.16 for 30 years.

$$\$539.16 \times 360 \text{ months} = \$194,097$$
$$\text{Less rent for same} \quad \underline{126,000}$$
$$\text{Difference} \quad \$\ 68,097$$

If you continue to rent, all you will have to show for that $126,000 is a very large pile of rent receipts. When you buy a house, however, you are investing your dollars and building your fixed assets. And the interest and taxes—every dollar paid—can be deducted yearly on your income tax report.

Although Mike and Lynn's problems prompted the research on this chapter, the dream of having your own home extends to most people—single or married. I checked with Mr. John Evans, an agent for a prominent real estate company to see if singles were active in buying property. He said that right now they represent less than 3 percent of the market. But, with careful planning, you could increase that statistic!

I know one young single man who saved enough to make a down payment on a townhouse. He moved in and piece by piece began to furnish it. A couple of years later, he married. His young bride moved in and they continued adding some of the things they wanted in their home. The value of the townhouse increased and in a couple of years they sold it, making a nice profit. His four year investment had paid off. Now they were ready to move into a larger house.

If you plan on buying a house with the thought of reselling it for a profit, you will need to allow at least three to five years for it to appreciate. Let's suppose you are going to make a 10 percent profit on the sale. That may sound great, but it will cost you 8.2 percent in salesman's commission and closing costs just to sell the house. And that is without paying points. With points, it will cost 11.8 percent. You would need 15 to 20 percent profit, at least, to make it worthwhile.

Buying a house is a good investment—as soon as you are ready to take on the payments and responsibility. But investigate all of the possibilities before signing that contract. As long as we have inflation, the house you buy this year will be worth more in the future.

I'm not going to tell you what kind of a house, old or new, to buy. Nor am I going to suggest the type of a loan you should consider. Let this chapter stimulate your thinking, though, and help you see the need to research the facts and make the wisest decision for you.

I want Mike and Lynn to have their dream house, but not before they are financially ready. If they go into it without the cash necessary to make the monthly payments fit comfortably into the budget, they will soon feel trapped with the responsibility of owning a house. They could even fall into the old pattern of charging the things they need—or want—because there is not enough income to cover it all.

If, however, they plan carefully and stay in control of their finances, they will *enjoy* the privileges and problems of being homeowners. I hope you will, too!

10/Looking For Alternatives Can Be Fun

There is more than one way to "skin a cat"—or to do almost anything in life. And, Mike and Lynn were busy discovering this. Their youthful ingenuity and imagination were hard at work. They were looking for another way of getting the money to tie down that new apartment—without waiting for the "due process" of the bright red budget book!

Too excited to wait for our regular Friday meeting, Mike called me at home one evening.

"Hi!" his voice boomed over the telephone. "Guess what?"

Almost afraid to find out, I said, "I can't imagine, Mike. Tell me."

"Do you remember that old watch I bought in Germany? Well, I sold it."

"That's great, Mike. What did you do with the money?" I hastened to ask.

"Oh, we put it in the bank," he said. "But that isn't all."

"You mean there's more?"

"Yes," he rushed on. "Remember that old hide-a-bed we had in our other apartment? We sold that, too."

Before I could slip a word in edgewise, he added, "And, a fellow at work is going to buy our old black and white TV set. He's going to give me the money payday."

Silence. He had either run out of breath—or old items to sell.

"Mike, I'm proud of you. What made you think of selling those things?" I asked.

Then he explained what I had already guessed.

"We're anxious to decide on an apartment and we thought that if we could come up with the deposit and one month's rent before payday, we could have it all ready to move into by the first of the month. And—the rent money that's already in the budget can be used to pay bills."

"Good thinking, Mike," I said.

"We have found one we like," he added, "but we'd like your opinion. Will you go with us to look at it?"

We did look at the apartment. They had done a good job. It was lovely: two bedrooms, gold carpeting and gold appliances. Just right for their furniture. They chose one on the garden level. It was considerably less expensive than the first and second floor apartments. And, best of all, it fit into the budget. Mike proudly paid the deposit. They could move in in two weeks.

The fulfillment of their first—and immediate—goal was just around the corner. They were on cloud nine.

Perhaps you are thinking, "But, I don't have any old furniture or antique watches to sell." It really doesn't matter. Raising money through a "second-hand business" is not the moral of this story. But looking for alternatives is. It can be the difference between being miserable and having fun during your financial crunch and recovery.

You can, of course, force yourself to "endure to the end," indulging in self-pity every inch of the way. But I hope you won't. The idea of looking for another way of doing things can be applied to almost anything. It adds a spark of adventure and fun to life—while you are learning to say, "I can't afford it."

If what you want to buy—or do—is too expensive for your budget, look for the alternative. Be careful, though, that the "other way" isn't just as costly. There are times when the best alternative is simply doing without.

Think about this. People who are miserable are usually unhappy with themselves. If you are keeping pace with Mike and Lynn, the worry and frustration of unpaid debts have been replaced with a planned recovery. You are now in control of your battered finances. Not out of debt, but in control. This should make you feel good about yourself.

And, while you are teaching yourself all of these character-building lessons, you can stop taking life and *things* for granted, and start having the time of your life discovering the simple joys in the world around you.

One day at lunch, Mike was telling me about a book he was reading. It included ideas on ways husbands could keep their wives happy.

"There was one great idea," he related, "and when I can afford it, I'm going to do it for Lynn. You make a coupon book and write individual coupons for things that you think your wife would like."

Intrigued, I asked, "What kind of things?"

"Well, for example, it suggested one coupon that would read, 'Good for $50 and a day free to go shopping. Babysitting provided.' Another one was, 'Good for one dinner date with your husband at your favorite restaurant.'"

"That sounds like fun, but why wait until you can afford it?" I asked.

"What do you mean?" Mike asked with interest.

"It's part of a game called 'looking for alternatives.'" I replied.

"Go on, I'm listening," Mike said, beginning to see the light.

"All right, Mike. How about these?"

- Good for one breakfast in bed on the day of your choice.
- Good for one deluxe shampoo.
- Good for one large pizza on a night when you least feel like cooking.
- Good for one backrub when you are especially tired.

"Wow! I see what you mean. I can use the same idea, but make out coupons that cost very little or nothing in the way of money."

It would be just as much fun if the coupon book was given by the wife to the husband. This idea can also be used by singles who are short on funds. How about a coupon book for your mom or dad? Your sister, brother, or a good friend? It could make a very thoughtful—and inexpensive—mother's day, father's day, or birthday gift.

Mike had an opportunity to practice this principle the very next day. He and Lynn had stopped by my office to talk about the move into their new apartment.

"I'll have to get some new bookcases," Mike announced. He had discarded the old metal ones when they moved out of the other apartment.

Lynn looked horrified, and I quickly interjected, "Mike, you can't *afford* new bookcases."

He got the point and quickly agreed. All of the beautiful books that had been piling up from those four book clubs would just have to stay in their boxes for a little longer—or would they?

"Mike," I asked, "isn't there another way to get bookcases without buying them?"

We all began to think.

Finally, Mike said, "We could make them."

"Yes, but out of what?" Lynn asked.

Turning to Mike, I said, "Would cinder blocks work for the ends?" I had just remembered a few extras in my basement.

They took over from there!

Mike said, "My dad has some old pieces of lumber in the garage."

Lynn added, "And my dad will let us use his electric sander."

Mike went to work. He cut the boards to size and gave them a thorough sanding. Then with a can of white spray paint for the cinder blocks, and a can of varnish for the shelves, he turned out a handsome set of book shelves for their new apartment—and all those books. The budget wasn't disturbed and the alternate idea more than satisfied the need.

This system—looking for alternatives—takes a little practice, but before long you will begin bumping into ideas everywhere you turn.

How about the entertainment areas or the leisure hours in your life? Will it work there? Absolutely.

Here are a few ideas to start your mental wheels turning:

A walk, hand-in-hand in the rain,
  the wind,
    the snow,
      the sunlight—or the moonlight.
A rousing game of tennis,
  Frisbee,
    Monopoly with friends,
      Checkers or chess for two, or any other
      no-cost game.

A picnic in the park,
  the country, the beach,
    the mountains,
      the backyard—the frontyard,
        or in the middle of the living room floor.
How about a pot-luck dinner
  with another couple,
    your neighbors,
      someone who is lonely,
        or even your family?
Do you have bicycles? Ride them
  around the lake,
    the block,
      through the park,
or any other place bikes can go.

I have a single friend at work who loves to climb rocks—big ones! But her girlfriends don't care for this activity, so she goes climbing with the fellows at church (who provide all of the equipment) when they invite her to join them. This may not appeal to you, but there are many no-cost, or low-cost, pleasures just waiting to be discovered.

We haven't even mentioned sharing a good book, or seeing your hometown through the eyes of a tourist. I have actually lived in Denver all of my life and have never paid a visit to the mint! Nor have I secured a pass to sit in on a session of the Colorado State House or Senate. The possibilities for such activities are unlimited. They are right at your doorstep.

I promise that whether you are single, married,

young or not-so-young, you can have fun looking for alternatives once you have developed the habit. And, when you have, you will discover that the most expensive way of doing—or buying—is not always the best, or the most fun!

Remember Paul? "... for I have learned, in whatever state I am, in this to be content."

Enjoy yourselves on the road to a balanced budget! You may look back someday and remember these as some of the happiest days of your life.

11/An Intelligent Approach to Insurance

I recently interviewed a fine Christian man, Darrell Baugh, who has been an insurance broker for over twenty-five years. He is now head of the National Estate Planning Institute in Boulder, Colorado. Admitting that I knew little or nothing about insurance, I turned to him for help. Mike and Lynn needed wise counsel. And he was qualified to give it.

He told me the insurance world has changed almost 180 degrees in the last ten years—and is still changing. I asked him if he could help me give Mike and Lynn and other young people an intelligent approach to insurance. Here is what he said:

"Just about everyone is confused by and about insurance. So let me state, in my own terms, the basic concept of all insurance:

"Insurance is an arrangement whereby an individual joins with a large group of people so that they can *all share each other's financial risk*. Each individual pays "dues" in the form of a premium. The premium is intended to provide the large group with sufficient funds to pay for the financial losses of each individual in the group. You may arrange to transfer most of your financial risk to the group—or you may retain a portion of the risk. The more risk you transfer to the group, the more premium you will have to pay. The more risk you retain, the lower your premium—but the more it will hurt you if the insured event happens."

I asked Mr. Baugh to explain what he meant by "retain a portion of the risk."

"I happen to believe in fairly high deductibles in car, home and health insurance. I insure 'the high end' of insurance risks. My cars, for instance, have a $500 deductible in the event of a collision. If I have a wreck, I will have to pay the first $500 of the repair bill. Sure, that $500 will hurt. But I try to drive carefully—and in all these years, I have never had a collision. And by 'self-insuring' the first $500, I can reduce my insurance bill by about $200 per year, per car. On the other hand, I carry the maximum liability coverage because I couldn't financially handle a $1,000,000 lawsuit. I have, essentially, the same philosophy regarding home and health insurance."

Perhaps you should consider your driving record. If you are accident prone, you probably wouldn't go this route. Or if someone in your family is a high-risk medically, you would want the most total coverage possible. It is, however, something you should consider.

Mr. Baugh went on to say: "There are some 2,000 life insurance companies in the United States. In addition, there are numerous companies that offer other kinds of insurance (auto, home, health, disability, liability, marine, industrial, etc., etc.). It is quite likely that the various plans offered by all of these companies would run well into the tens of thousands of plans. No wonder people are confused. The insurance companies, however, did not design these plans in order to confuse the buying public. The plans were designed to meet the varying needs of the public. When placed in the hands of a skillful, professional insurance agent or broker, the plans can be applied in a way that will meet the needs of the insurance buyer at the best price.

"No person can possibly know all of the various plans available. Some people seem to think that it is a grand idea to have one insurance agent or broker handle all of their insurance needs. It does simplify the question of where to go if you have a claim. But the chances are that you will not get the best insurance coverage at the best price if you have only one person or agency handling all of your insurance needs. The reason is simple: they do not represent all of the various companies. They cannot possibly know all of the various plans available to meet your needs."

Insurance representatives come in two broad, basic categories: *agents* and *brokers*.

Agents are persons who are licensed by the various states to represent an insurance company to the buying public. The agent is primarily a salesperson for a particular insurance company.

A *broker* is a person licensed by the states to represent the buyer to the insurance companies. Depending upon your circumstances, this can be an important difference.

As Mr. Baugh explained, "An agent is likely to have a more complete knowledge of his company's plans and procedures. If that company does not have a plan that meets your needs specifically, though, the agent would be restricted in his ability to provide the proper insurance plan. A broker, on the other hand, has a large number of companies to choose from and is more likely to be able to meet your needs. However, the broker is less likely to know all of a given company's plans and procedures.

"Don't be afraid to shop among insurance companies. There are some enormous differences between insurance companies and their plans and their premium rates. You should shop for insurance the way you shop for a car or clothes. Don't be impressed by computer printouts or bells and whistles!

"The A.M. Best Company of Oldwick, New Jersey, has served as an independent analyst of various insurance companies for the past eighty years or so. Their ratings are issued much like school grades (A+, A, B-, etc.). Each company should be willing to tell you what their "Best's Report" is. Ask the agent or broker about the "Best Report" or "Best's Rating" for any company proposed to you. Don't be afraid to ask, 'Why should I pay you more money than Company A? What am I getting for that extra money?' Generally, you can feel very safe with a company with a Best Rating of A+ or A."

How do you actually select an agent or broker for your various insurance needs? Mr. Baugh suggested:

1. Ask your parents who they use for the various insurance coverages that you need: their auto insurance broker; their life insurance representative. Ask if they are pleased with the person as an individual. If your parents are satisfied, the chances are good that you will be, too.
2. Ask your employer. If your parents do not live in the same area you do, your employer might be a good source for reputable agents or brokers. If you work for a very large company, it might be impractical to ask the company president, so ask your supervisor. At least ask someone who has experience in this area.
3. Ask for referrals from friends. This may be a less reliable method of finding a good agent—but it may beat walking through the Yellow Pages. One question to ask your friends when they are giving you the name of their favorite insurance agent, is this: 'Is this person a really good insurance agent—or is this person a good friend?' You want a good agent.
4. There are some measurement devices to help insurance buyers know the educational background of an insurance agent. For instance:

a) CLU—Chartered Life Underwriter. This person is generally an expert in the field of life and/or health insurance.
b) RHU—Registered Health Underwriter. This person is usually proficient in the field of health, major medical and disability income insurance.
c) CPCU—Chartered Property and Casualty Underwriter. This is the professional designation for those who deal in home and automobile insurance matters.
d) LUTCF—Life Underwriter Training Council Fellow, another designation for the life and health insurance business.

Mr. Baugh concluded by saying, "The most important thing for people like Mike and Lynn—or you or me—is to find insurance advisors who are knowledgeable, and who are willing to be in our corner. It is important that you have the insurance you need—but *only* what you need and at the best prices available."

There are five kinds of insurance that you will want to consider. They are:

    Medical Insurance
    Automobile Insurance
    Home Owner's Insurance/Renter's Insurance
    Life Insurance
    Disability Income Insurance

With the inflationary spiral of hospital and medical expenses today, it is important to be covered with a good *medical insurance policy*.

Mike and Lynn have coverage under the group plan where he works. The amount is automatically deducted from his salary once a month. (We didn't even list it in their budget.)

Due to complications when little Bobby was born, Mike and Lynn had over $6,000 in hospital and doctor bills in one year. Without medical insurance, it would have been a financial disaster. It will, however, be ten years before they will have paid that much in insurance payments.

If your employer has a group plan for health insurance, be sure you are enrolled. Find out when the coverage goes into effect and any waiting period there might be for certain types of care. Read the fine print for any exclusions such as pregnancy. Group coverage is usually better and also less expensive than an individual policy. Don't put this off. Youth is no guarantee against accident or illness. And, even a brief stay in the hospital can cost thousands of dollars.

Automobile insurance is probably the first kind of insurance you were introduced to—on the day you started driving your own car. Banks and lending agencies require this coverage while you are paying for your car. Unless you can afford expensive insurance, it is wise to stay away from expensive cars. You will need coverage for Liability, Property Damage and Personal Injury which are required by law in most states.

Rates are usually determined by your age, your driving record, the kind of car you drive, and the coverage you desire. Usually you have your choice of paying once a year or every six months. The twice a year payment plan is easier to fit into a tight budget. Some companies will even allow you to pay monthly or quarterly. Be sure to check the rates on these. They may be higher.

Home Owner's Insurance is required by the bank holding the mortgage on your house. It protects you—and the bank—against loss by fire, lightning, theft, vandalism, etc. This is a part of your P.I.T.I. monthly house payments.

If you are renting an apartment, townhouse, or house, you may want to consider *household content insurance.* The only difference between this and the home owner's policy is that it does not cover the dwelling. It only covers the contents. For this reason it is much less expensive.

Life Insurance is a more complex package, partly because there are so many different plans and combinations to be considered. Your insurance program should be tailored for you and your family. Some general information may help you ask the right questions and be prepared to judge the value of various insurance proposals.

Two important questions you should ask yourself as you buy life insurance are:

(1) What will the needs of my family be if I should die prematurely, or become disabled?

(2) What can I afford to pay for this coverage?

Remember, you can always add additional insurance as your income increases in future years.

There are two basic types of life insurance offered. We'll just touch on these. They are *permanent* life insurance and *term* life insurance.

There are four popular permanent life insurance plans. These plans guarantee the rates at the age and date of issue. The premiums remain the same for the life of the policy. These plans also create cash and loan values for future years.

Plan One: Whole, or Straight, Life Insurance
The premiums on this plan continue as long as the insured lives. It can be cashed in at any time. The premiums are usually lower than the other plans.

Plan Two: Limited Life Plan
This policy is *paid up* in a specific number of years. The premiums stop at this point and the face value of the policy is held by the insurance company as a death benefit.

Plan Three: Endowment Plan
The difference between this plan and the Limited Life Plan is that when it matures, the face value is paid to the insured and the policy canceled.

Plan Four: Universal Life
This policy combines term insurance with current financial inventory. Premium rates are flexible above a certain minimum amount. That minimum amount is generally higher than straight term insurance. This policy has the *potential* to build a higher cash value than ordinary life of the same premium. It does require physical qualification.

Now, let's take a look at term insurance. It should definitely be considered by young couples just starting out. The premiums are low and the coverage is high. One other advantage is that it can be converted later to a permanent plan—and the insurance company guarantees the best rate at the time of conversion. Here are four plans under term insurance:

Plan One: Group Term Life Insurance

Many businesses offer this group coverage for their employees. The rates are low and the policy is in effect as long as the individual is employed by the company. No physical qualification is required.

Plan Two: Level Term Insurance

This policy is taken out by an individual for a specific period of time. It may be renewed in one-year or five-year increments, or converted to a permanent plan. The premium will increase, however, to agree with the rate for the current age of the insured. For young people, the increase could be as small as one percent. Later in life, it can be as much as fifteen percent. Some type of physical qualification is required.

Plan Three: Reducing Term Insurance

This is much the same as the Level Term Plan, except the face value decreases and the premium remains the same.

Plan Four: Joint-Term Policy

With this plan, the husband and the wife are both insured under one policy. This would be wise if both are working. It could be equally important if there are children. If either parent were to die prematurely, the other would not be thrown into some kind of catastrophic situation.

There is also a term rider which can be added to a permanent policy. You may wish to start with a small amount of permanent, low premium insurance with a sizable term rider. Later, when your income increases and you are established in your career, you can convert the term insurance to a larger, permanent plan.

Disability Income Insurance may not seem too important when you are young and strong. However, according to Mr. Baugh, a male aged 35 or younger is approximately *five times* more likely to become disabled than he is to die prior to age 65! This insurance—if not provided by your employer— is something you should consider.

There are a few things you should *not* buy from an insurance agent if you are a young single person or a young couple.

A Retirement Plan: This is premature since careers are not yet established and cash will be needed to start a savings program and pay off obligations for the things needed to settle your home. We will touch on this in the next chapter, "Planning for the Future."

Insurance on a Financed Plan: In other words, do not sign a promissory note to pay insurance premiums. Most State Insurance Departments allow this and many companies encourage this practice, but it is dangerous. There is little, or no cash value in the early years of a life insurance policy and you stand to lose nearly all of your dollar investment when you are forced to pay the note plus the interest.

Accidental Death Clause: Young people, especially, seem to think that they are more likely to die by accidental means. Because of this, they sometimes opt for the lower premiums on a policy with a lower face value, but with this clause which is also known as "double indemnity." This means the policy will pay off at twice the face value if the insured dies in an accidental manner. But families like Mike, Lynn and Bobby need a certain amount of life insurance. The cause of death will not change that need. Fathers and mothers should not leave their families dependent upon a form of insurance that may not pay off because they died the wrong way. Insurance companies know what they are doing, but, in general, double indemnity is not a good bargain.

Waiver of Premium Benefits: This allows the insurance company to waive the premium during the total disability of the insured. The interpretation of disability is very restrictive—and the cost of this benefit is quite high in comparison to its true benefit. While this is a form of disability income insurance, it is *the* most costly form of insurance for this purpose! It would be far better to buy more regular disability income insurance.

Remember, the most important thing is to find insurance advisers who are knowledgeable and willing to be in the buyer's corner. It is crucial to have the insurance you need—but *only* what you need at the best prices possible.

Planning for the future is important, and Mr. Baugh is going to help us plan an intelligent insurance program for Mike and Lynn in the next chapter. And since you—and Mike and Lynn—are not always going to be in financial chaos, we will also do a little financial planning for "down the road!"

12/Planning for the Future

The "future" can mean tomorrow, next week, next year, or way down the road. No one knows what the future holds. The Apostle James put it clearly in James 4:13-15:

"[Come] now, ye that say, Today or tomorrow we will go into such a city, and continue there a year, and buy and sell, and get gain; Whereas ye know not what shall be on the next day. For what is your life? It is even a vapor that appeareth for a little time, and then vanisheth away. For ye ought to say, If the Lord will, we shall live, and do this, or that."

This Scripture does not mean we should have no plan. It does mean that our planning for the future should be done according to God's will for our lives.

Some plans for the future are exciting. Like Mike and Lynn's plans to move into their new apartment, or planning a trip or a party. Planning is also wise. It's the smart thing to do.

The first wise thing we are going to look at is a "Last Will and Testament." You are probably thinking, "Now, wait a minute! We're young! We don't need a will."

Wrong! Young people die every day.

Property held as "joint tenant with right of survivorship" will automatically pass to the surviving owner. Couples, however, should still have a will in case both die at the same time, perhaps in an accident.

Even single people need a simple will. You may have a car, furniture, jewelry, savings, etc. What happens if you die? Family members can divide it up or fight over it. Or the state can step in and decide. How much better if you make your wishes known through a will.

In her column, "Your Money Matters," Karen Slater writes, "Some attorneys and financial planners have a simple but effective strategy for prodding clients to write wills: They give them a copy of the 'will' dictated by the laws of their state for a person who dies without one."

Theodore E. Hughes, an assistant attorney general in Michigan says, "Even if you have nothing, you should still have a will to select who would be guardian of the minor children."

Mr. Baugh goes a step farther. He says that the minute the wife becomes pregnant, the prospective parents should have a will drawn up to specify who they wish to raise their child should anything happen to both parents.

A will is also important for single parents. There are cases where the parent who does not have custody of the children would be an unwise choice as guardian should the parent with custody die. When a will exists, the court will *usually* go along with the wishes included in the will. If no will exists, the court will almost always give custody to the surviving parent or another family member.

Mr. Baugh told me a beautiful story about his own family. When his children were eight and twelve, he and his wife decided they should rewrite their will to provide guardianship for their children. They didn't have any family members they wished to raise them, so they selected three families from among their friends. Families with the *same set of values* as theirs. They talked this over with the children.

They said, "We are not planning on dying in the near future, but if God in his infinite wisdom, should call us home at the same time, we want to be sure you are well cared for."

They went on to say, "Here are three families that you know well. Of these three, which would you prefer to be your foster parents."

The children left the room to talk it over. They came back and told their parents which family they wanted. The family was contacted and enthusiastically accepted the responsibility. The two families got together over dinner to openly discuss this arrangement. Mr. Baugh said there was a very special bond between his children and the other family from that time on.

He told his children, "If the time should come and we don't return home, pack your bags. Your new family will be coming to pick you up."

There are lawyers who advertise simple wills for around $45. If provision for guardianship is included, it will probably add another $15 or $20. If, like Mike and Lynn, you absolutely cannot afford to go to an attorney at this time, standard "Last Will and Testament" forms are available at your local office supply store. These can be purchased for less than a dollar. You will need to have it notarized, and this can run from free to $3 depending on where you go. Even Mike and Lynn could handle that! You will need two witnesses besides the notary. A personally done will is better than no will at all. It can be presented in court, and your wishes will be made known.

This is something you can do right in the middle of your financial crisis. And it is important! And as soon as you can afford it, have an attorney rewrite your will to be sure it covers everything necessary.

The next thing you can do is find wise insurance coverage at a very low cost. Mr. Baugh is going to walk us through a simple exercise that will help Mike and Lynn decide how much insurance they will need.

First, we have to determine what Mike and Lynn want to care for in the event of Mike's premature death. Let's make a list:

Final expenses. These are usually around $5,000 and this would not be an overstatement in Mike and Lynn's case. But, let's be conservative and make it $3,000.

Education. When small children are involved, it is certainly not unusual to set aside some money for an educational fund. It can be whatever Mike and Lynn want it to be. Some fix the cost of a college education at $60,000. But there are less expensive colleges, so let's make it $20,000. This is not out of line.

A Mortgage Fund. Even though Mike and Lynn do not own a home at this time, they probably will. It would be wise to cover this. If Mike were to die, Lynn could buy a house, or pay off the mortgage, or use the money for some other purpose. We'll list this at $60,000.

An Emergency Fund. In the event of Mike's death, this is something that will keep all the rest of this from coming apart if an emergency does arise. $10,000 would not be unusual. Until it is needed, Lynn can set it aside in some sort of investment program.

Assuming that Mike's take-home pay is $1,200 per month, this is the amount Lynn and Bobby would need in hard income if he were to die. We also need to keep in mind that in this event, their health insurance would no longer be in effect and Lynn would have to buy that on her own.

Let's see what we have:

Final expenses	$ 3,000
Education Fund	20,000
Mortgage Fund	60,000
Emergency Fund	10,000
Total	$93,000

If Bobby were three years old when Mike dies, he and Lynn would qualify for Social Security for the next fifteen years. Let's set Mike's gross income at $1500 per month. Looking at today's Social Security tables for a surviving spouse and one child, they would receive about $780 per month. Since Lynn needs $1200 per month, we subtract the $780 to find the additional income she will need. If your arithmetic is the same as mine, she will need $420.

She will need some type of interest income that will pay $420 per month. Let's choose a conservative interest rate, say 8%. Lynn will need $63,000 to net the $420.

Let's put it together:

Insurance needs	$ 93,000
Investment......................	63,000
Total	$156,000

Now, let's see what they already have. Mike would probably have some life insurance coverage from the company where he works. Let's assume it is $15,000. Perhaps his folks bought a life insurance policy on him for $1,000. Since they have no other assets, they will need an additional $140,000 of insurance on Mike to cover these needs in the event of his death. All of these needs should be tied together in the same plan. For example, an individual mortgage policy can often be too expensive. Also, burial insurance by itself is terribly expensive.

Checking one insurance company's rates, Mike

could buy term insurance of $140,000 for about $16.70 per month. This would go up every year, or every five years, depending on the policy. Mike and Lynn can easily afford to have this kind of coverage, and they need it now—even while they are over their heads in debt. It will make Lynn's and Bobby's futures secure.

The will and the insurance are protections Mike and Lynn can have immediately. You can, too. Your insurance agent or broker can help you with an exercise like this to determine the amount of insurance you need.

Now, let's plan for "down the road."

We need to plan for a future—*with* Mike. When Mike and Lynn are ready—out of debt, intelligently insured and ready to build for that future—they need to consider seeing a financial planner. And just as you want to select your insurance representative with care, you also want to shop for a reputable financial planner.

A good financial planner will start with the assets you already have, find out where you want to go, and discover your emotional feelings about money and investments. He will help you build a financial plan that will be just right for you. For example, I am a bit chicken when it comes to investing hard-earned dollars in something that is risky. On the other hand, I want to earn the highest interest rate possible. I want growth—and security. And, there is even a plan for someone like me.

Mr. Baugh explained that most financial planners use a "pyramid" format. Here is an example:

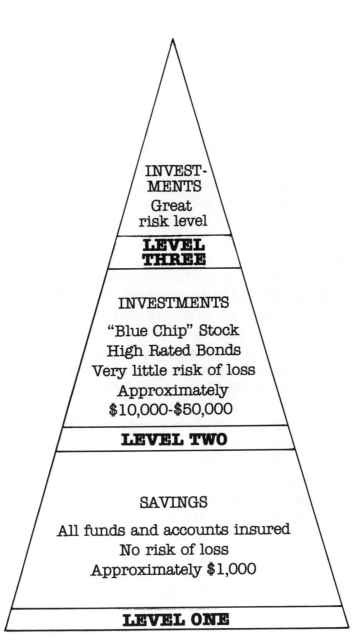

INVEST-
MENTS
Great
risk level

LEVEL THREE

INVESTMENTS

"Blue Chip" Stock
High Rated Bonds
Very little risk of loss
Approximately
$10,000-$50,000

LEVEL TWO

SAVINGS

All funds and accounts insured
No risk of loss
Approximately $1,000

LEVEL ONE

The first block in the pyramid represents your savings. You should set this at least at $1,000. This should be in insured funds and accounts. No risk of loss! (This goes back to our savings account number one.) Anything over and above this amount falls into the second block of the pyramid. These dollars are to be invested in something with very little or no risk. $10,000 is a good goal to start, but you can set it as high as you want.

The peak of the pyramid adds an interesting dimension to your financial plan. Here, you can determine the amount you want to put into a high-yield, high-risk type of investment. The secret is to invest only what you can *afford* to lose! Never more than that, and not before the other two blocks are securely in place.

Any financial planning you do when you are young will help you prepare for that far distant future—retirement!

There are many companies which have retirement programs for their employees. But you have no guarantee that you will still be working for that company when the time comes to retire. And Social Security, as glad as we are to have it, does not pay enough to have the kind of retirement you see advertised in the travel magazines. You need more.

If income taxes are a problem and you need a tax break, you might want to consider an IRA (Individual Retirement Act) account. The amount you invest each year comes right off the top of your taxable income.

I like IRAs. I like the tax break, and I have many choices where I can invest my money. Doing a little research at my local bank, Sandra Thompson, an IRA representative, agreed to answer some questions for me. Here is some of the information she gave me:

- Most institutions require only $100 to open an IRA account. Some credit unions will open one for as little as $25.
- You can add as little as $25 a month after that. In some cases even less.
- The most you can deposit in a year is $2,000.
- The average age for opening an account is 30-35 years. Many of these are singles.
- Any money withdrawn from your IRA account, before age 59½, will suffer an interest penalty.
- Whenever money is withdrawn, it will be taxed.
- IRA investments can be made in money market accounts; mutual funds; stocks; bonds; certificates of deposit—almost any form of investment.

Sandra gave me a copy of a chart that shows the advantages of investing in a tax sheltered plan, such as an IRA account, as opposed to a taxable savings plan.

INDIVIDUAL RETIREMENT ACCOUNT
(Illustration of a savings account @ 8% compounded annually)

$2,000 deposited at beginning of each year in IRA
$1,500 deposited in savings account

| | | Value at 8% at age 65 | |
Starting age	Total deposit age 65	With IRA	Without IRA Tax bracket 25%
60	$10,000	$ 12,672	$ 8,963
55	20,000	31,290	20,957
50	30,000	58,648	37,009
45	40,000	98,423	58,489
40	50,000	157,908	87,234
35	60,000	244,692	125,700
30	70,000	372,204	177,181
25	80,000	599,562	246,072

The above table assumes an investor took $2,000 (with an IRA), or $1,500 (25% tax bracket) and put it in a savings account at 8%, compounded annually. Without IRA, 25% is deducted annually from net income to pay taxes. A savings account has been selected because it is a frequently used and widely known medium of savings. Interest is considered to be relatively stable and principal is guaranteed by the savings institution. These results should not be considered representative of an actual Individual Retirement Account; the comparison is only intended to illustrate the advantage of having a tax shelter over that of a non-shelter plan.

122

You should be familiar with this as a possible part of your financial pyramid.

Mike and Lynn are not ready to invest in much of anything right now. And, unlike their will and insurance needs which are immediate, their visit to a financial planner can be put off until they are ready.

Right now they need to know the joy of bills that are marked "paid."

13/The Joy of a Bill Marked "Paid"

Another Friday evening, only this time I was standing outside the door of Mike and Lynn's new apartment. They had invited me to dinner—and tomorrow was payday.

Four short months had slipped by, almost unnoticed, since Mike and I had had our first meeting. It didn't seem possible! So much had happened. They had completed their counseling with the pastor; they were back together as a family—and they were in control of their personal finances.

With my finger on the doorbell, I hesitated just a moment to say, "Thank you, Lord, for everything!"

I pushed the doorbell. The door opened and there stood Mike and Lynn—looking so *right*. And, from his room came little Bobby on the run, grinning from ear to ear. Once again, everything was all right in his world.

I was barely inside when Mike asked, "Shall we eat first, or pay bills?"

Mike would rather eat than almost anything, so I knew something in that budget book had him excited. Then, I remembered. The extra money from the rent was burning a hole in his checkbook!

I glanced at Lynn's beautiful table. The candles were already lit.

"Let's eat first," I said. "The budget will wait."

It was a happy dinner—Lynn's individual meatloaves were just perfect. She gave me a knowing smile as she served Mike his.

Almost as fast as Lynn and I cleared the table, Mike arrived from the other room with the checkbook, the budget book and his trusty little calculator. This time we were around *their* table.

"What shall we do with the extra money?" Mike began.

"Why don't we pay our regular bills first, Mike?" Lynn suggested. "And when we know how much is left, we can decide the best place to put it, okay?"

Mike laughed. "Sure," he said. "That makes sense. I'm just so anxious to see what we can accomplish with it."

He handed Lynn the checkbook and she began writing the checks. As Mike made the entries and checked off each item in the budget book, he said, "You know, this bright red budget book is becoming a way of life."

"That's the idea," I replied.

The key to good money management is consistency. Once you have built your payment schedule, stick to it. Of course, you will need to adjust it as you review your priorities from time to time. Circumstances have a way of changing these.

Before long, though, you will be paying off some of your bills. This will free those dollars to be used, or invested, someplace else. Don't let them slip through your fingers! Decide immediately where you want to reschedule them.

This may be the time you will want to increase your giving; double up on another debt; open a savings account—or perhaps all three depending on the amount you have to work with.

It was gratifying to see that Mike was thinking along these lines. He had their short-term goals clearly in focus.

When all of the bills were paid, and the last item was checked off in the budget book, Mike totaled the checks written and gave us the amount left. They both looked at me—waiting for me to suggest where to put the extra money. Instead of telling them where I thought it should go, I said, "Why don't you turn to your 'Record of Progress' section and take a look at all seven accounts. Then, *you* decide where the wisest payment could be made."

Mike had learned what to look for when he had the $135 left after that $30 dinner and the book club payments!

But would he remember?

Even little birds have to be pushed out of the nest if they are going to learn to fly on their own—and it was about time to test Mike and Lynn's wings.

They began studying each account. Mike seemed to be thinking out loud, but Lynn was listening. This was her first exposure to this kind of reasoning.

"Hm-m-m, the largest balance is still on Visa, but

the monthly payment is only $37. If we pay it here, the balance will be lower, but we would still have the payment in the budget."

Then he turned back to Department Store #1.
"On the other hand—this account has a fixed payment of $50 and..."

Now he was getting excited.
"...and—with the regular payment we just made—WE COULD WIPE IT OUT!"

He calmed down just a bit and explained to Lynn, "This would eliminate $50 from the payment schedule and free that much for..."

He stopped.
I laughed and said, "Mike you did it! That's exactly what I would have suggested."

Handing the checkbook back to Lynn, he said, "Man, you have to think these things through, don't you?"

Lynn gleefully wrote out the check while Mike entered the extra payment on the "Record of Progress" page for Department Store #1. This was their first "zero" balance. With a flourish he wrote, "Paid in Full," across the page—and signed his name.

"I think we should all autograph this page," he said, and handed the book to Lynn.
Laughing with excitement, Lynn added her name and handed the book across the table to me.

DEPARTMENT STORE #1

Date				Fin. Chg.		Payment	Balance
		Starting balance					48000
12/15				5	92	5000	43592
1/15				5	49	18500	25641
2/15				5	06	5000	21147
3/15				4	60	5000	16607
4/15				4	23	5000	12030
4/15						12030	-0-

PAID IN
FULL
//

Mike
Amy & Lynn

128

Oh, the joy of a bill marked, "Paid."

One down—and six to go.

In the beginning of this book, I warned you that it would not present a highly technical budget program. And, of course, it doesn't, but I hope you are catching the spirit of excitement, and yes, even the fun, of gaining control of your unruly finances. Once you are out of debt, you may want to move on to a more detailed, sophisticated plan. And, that is fine. The important thing is that you continue having a plan!

It's easy to slip into old habits. Remember the self-control you have exercised and continue to pay bills *first* and then decide what to do with the balance. Don't run the risk of a repeat performance.

"Where shall we schedule the extra $50?" Lynn wanted to know.

"It won't appear in the budget again until next month," I said, "so why don't we wait until then to decide? By then you will know if we have allowed enough for your regular living expenses."

"It *was* hard to make the grocery money stretch this last payday," she admitted.

When Mike and Lynn moved into the new apartment, their living expenses increased overnight. The budget didn't allow room in which to even wiggle. They needed a bit more breathing space.

But there was another large expense looming on the horizon. As much as we all, especially Mike, wished it would just go away, we knew it wouldn't. Sooner or later it would have to be faced.

Mike needed extensive dental work. It had already been postponed too long. Increasingly, Mike appeared with a swollen face from a painful tooth. He hated to bring the subject out in the open.

"I have an appointment to see a dentist next week," he admitted reluctantly. "We may need it to make the payments on that bill."

Mike and Lynn were not going to be free from financial pressures for a long time, but together they were learning to handle them bravely, efficiently—and with contentment.

The joy of that first bill marked, "Paid," was just the encouragement they needed!

14/Cutting The Budget Pie Into Pieces

The happy payday arrived when Mike and Lynn were able to pay off Department Store #2. I was delighted to hear Mike say, "Let's add $5 a payday to our giving."

The balance of that payment would go toward the other charge accounts. The "Record of Progress" section in the budget book was the visual proof that Mike and Lynn were gaining on those seven charge accounts.

Anticipating a debt-free future, Lynn said, "We were reading an article the other day about setting up a budget on percentages. Would that give us the guidelines necessary to keep this from ever happening again?"

Let's find out.

If you have read many articles or books on the management of personal finances, you no doubt have run into this theory. The most popular breakdown seems to be the 10-20-70 percentage scale, or some list it as 10-70-20. Everyone seems to agree that the 70 percent is for "living expenses," and the 10 percent for "saving or investing."

One writer said the 20 percent was "yours to enjoy," while another designated it as a "debts and buffer fund." I have to admit that these figures sound great, but I also have to ask, "Are they practical?"

Will they work in today's inflationary economy?

In all the percentage charts I have seen, the 100 percent is based on your income after federal, state and Social Security taxes have been deducted. These are required by law. How much you pay is not your decision. The amount you receive in your check on payday, after taxes, is commonly called "take-home pay." To keep this clear, we will refer to income *before* taxes as "gross income," and *after* taxes as "net income."

If the article or book on finances is written from a Christian point of view, the 100 percent almost always begins after taxes and the tithe have been deducted. Let me hasten to say that I am not trying to debate the subject, but it does seem rather odd for a Christian to place the tithe in the same category with taxes. It makes the matter of giving an impersonal, automatic obligation with no place in your 100 percent budget plan.

This brings to the surface the two schools of thought on how the tithe should be figured. Many Christians firmly believe that the tithe should be based on the gross income. Others feel it should be calculated on the net income—take-home pay. The decision, I believe, rests solely between the individual and the Lord. The government, however, does allow you to claim up to thirty percent of your gross income for donations to charitable and religious organizations.

In our chapter on tithing, we found that our giving should come from a willing mind and a heart of love. If your giving is motivated by fear, it becomes a legal obligation. If you are motivated by love, it is a spiritual blessing and in times of prosperity, you will give—and give! When Christ is truly Lord of your life, you just naturally want to give all that you possibly can. The New Testament, however, also teaches that you are to give out of what you have and not out of what you do not have. Your giving has to be realistic.

We decided to take Mike and Lynn's income and apply the percentage system. We worked it up three ways just for fun! First, we took the total gross income to see what percent goes into taxes. The government took the top 20 percent of Mike's pay. We used the accepted 25 percent for housing. This has to include the principal, interest, taxes and insurance (P.I.T.I.) for a home. We added the 10 percent based on gross income for the tithe.

Since insurance seldom appears as a separate listing in percentage plans, we took Mike and Lynn's actual insurance amounts. They were medical insurance, automobile insurance and his life insurance. This took an 8 percent slice out of the budget pie.

Next, we added the 10 percent recommended for savings or investments. This is where the *two* savings accounts would come from. Add these up and you will discover that we have exactly 27 percent left to cover the following items:

Groceries	Doctor bills
Car payment	Medicine
Transportation	Recreation
Clothing	Miscellaneous

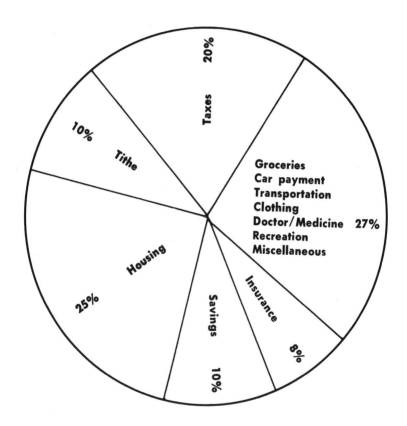

Total Gross Income

We had to abandon this pie in a hurry. There was no way that 27 percent could cover the above expenses. The only item on the list that some might question is the car payment. But, let's be realistic. Most young couples, and young singles, *are* paying for a car! In fact, at today's prices, most adults who drive a car are seldom without a car payment in the budget. And in most areas a car is a necessity.

Next, we made an "after tax and tithe pie." Here's how it turned out:

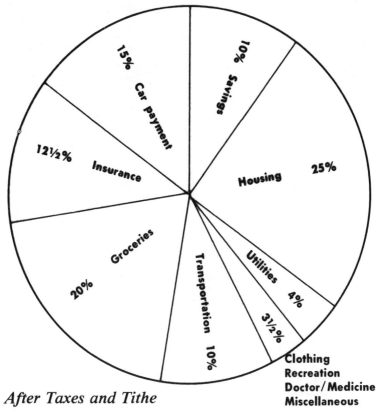

After Taxes and Tithe

135

This time, we ended up with 3½ percent to cover clothing, recreation, doctor bills, medicine and miscellaneous expenses. There was one problem, however. By applying the 25 percent for housing to their income after taxes and tithe, it allowed only $210 for this purpose. In most areas today, this is unrealistic. And, trying to buy a house with this amount for a monthly payment would be impossible.

Our next example consisted of the full take-home pay after taxes. The 25 percent for housing automatically went up to $240. In our inflation ridden economy, this is still not enough for the monthly payments on a house—or rent on an apartment—unless it is a very small house with a very large down payment!

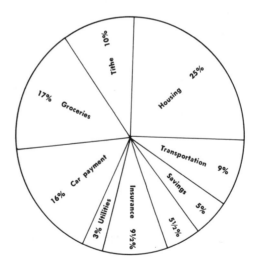

After Taxes—Net Income

You will also notice that we had to cut the savings to 5 percent. This left 5½ percent for clothing, recreation, doctor bills, medicine and miscellaneous expenses.

It is still tight. The solution, of course, is more income. When Mike gets his next raise in pay, it will automatically increase the amount of his taxes and tithe. However, since most entries are fixed amounts, their percentages will decrease as Mike's income increases. This will allow an added amount to go into savings.

Your percentage pie may be completely different from Mike and Lynn's, but then, no two pies ever come out exactly alike! I think you will find it interesting, though, to start with your total income and figure the percent that goes into taxes. Then, continue with your existing expenses.

Just in case your arithmetic is a bit rusty, here is how to arrive at your percentages. If your total income per month is $1200 and your food allowance is $200, just divide the larger amount into the smaller, like this:

$$1200 \overline{\smash{\big)}\, 200.00} \quad .16\,\tfrac{2}{3}$$

$$\begin{array}{r} .16\,\tfrac{2}{3} \\ 1200 \overline{\smash{\big)}\, 200.00} \\ \underline{120\ 0} \\ 80\ 00 \\ \underline{72\ 00} \\ 8\ 00 \end{array}$$

I'm not sure I could live with a percentage budget, but it does offer some excellent guidelines and warning signs. We'll list a few that Mike and Lynn found helpful.

1. In Exhibit #1, we discovered that 25 percent for housing took too big a bite out of the *total income pie.* Even though a bank will approve a mortgage loan on your new home if your gross income is four times the amount of the monthly P.I.T.I. payment, it could create a tight financial position. We decided a better scale would be from 20 to 25 percent *after* taxes.

2. We also discovered that it took 8 percent of Mike's total wages to provide wise insurance coverage. This included medical, automobile and life insurance. As their income increases, the first two will remain stable and they can then decide if it is time to increase their life insurance.

3. We decided that the percentages to watch and control were housing and insurance. And the percentages to be held and protected were the tithe and savings. In the day-to-day living expenses, it would still require wise spending—and sticking to the bright red budget book!

This leaves you with the decision regarding how you figure your tithe—on your before or after taxes income. Whatever your decision, I challenge you to put the Lord first in all of your finances. Everything you have, you have because He has made it possible. If you find that with your income and family responsibilities you can tithe your gross income, I heartily recommend it. However, if you are managing your income wisely and can't afford that amount, don't feel that less is wrong. Tithe your take-home pay and be willingly and lovingly faithful in your giving. You know in your heart what God expects from you.

15/Who Promised You a Rose Garden?

"I'm wondering just *what* it will take to upset you," Mike said with amazement, "or didn't you hear what I said?"

I had heard all right. Mike had just announced that his dental work was going to cost $3,000, and the dentist wanted cash after each session!

"Financial problems that you can't help won't phase me," I replied calmly. "We'll work them out somehow. But, you *create* one—and you'll find out what upsets me."

We laughed, for the thought of him spending even $1 that wasn't in the budget, at that moment, seemed impossible. Outside of that one $30 dinner, he had been nearly perfect.

I was calm on the outside, but inside I was thinking, "Three thousand dollars! It's like starting all over again."

I knew that root resections, extractions, partials and caps were expensive, but I had hoped for maybe $1,500. We would have to borrow it!

We made an appointment at the bank where Mike and Lynn had their checking account. The gentleman we talked with didn't hold out much hope, but he gave Mike the forms to fill out and return. As we left the bank, Mike said, "It's at a time like this I could wish we had a good credit rating."

There comes a time in almost everyone's life when it is necessary to borrow money. Keeping your personal finances in shape and maintaining a good credit record *are* essential. Mike was learning that the hard—and embarrassing—way.

The bank, of course, turned down the loan when it received their application and saw their financial statement. They were still paying on five charge accounts and one small car. However, if they could find someone who *could* qualify and was willing to co-sign the note, they could have the money. Parents, bless them, are often lifesavers. Within a week they had their $3,000, *after* I had assured the parents that the payments on the loan would fit into Mike and Lynn's bright red budget book!

What do do with so much money? We decided to put $2,500 of it into a savings account and withdraw it as needed. It would take at least three months for the dental work to be completed. The money could earn some interest and it would also be less tempting than it would be in the checking account.

Mike would owe $500 by next week, so this amount was deposited in the checking account. Even that amount seemed like a fortune.

The next day, after Mike and Lynn had been to the bank, they stopped by my office. I knew at once that something was wrong. Lynn was too quiet—

and Mike was too talkative! He took out his checkbook and explained a couple of small checks they had written. Just above those two checks, I noticed an unidentified entry for $9.50.

"What was the $9.50 check for?" I asked.

Lynn turned and walked to the other side of my office. Mike looked uncomfortable and then started to explain.

"You know those free gifts the bank gives when you open a savings account? Well—we didn't see anything we wanted in the free ones they offered. But you could get this pocket calculator for only $9.50 extra, so I bought it."

Now, I was upset!

They didn't have $9.50 to spend! And Mike already had a pocket calculator. It had been a regular attender at every one of our budget meetings.

For the next several minutes, I proceeded to remind Mike that buying on impulse was one of his basic problems; that he had agreed not to write any checks after payday without discussing it first; and—before I could offer to remove myself from his financial picture—Mike turned on his heel and walked out. Out of my office. Clear out of the building and into his car!

I felt terrible. And Lynn was crying.

"I tried to stop him from buying it," she said, "but he wouldn't listen to me. I cried all the way home."

That is what was bothering them when they first arrived. It was probably their first "misunderstanding" since they had gotten back together. And all over a measly $9.50!

Then I remembered.

Mike and Lynn were supposed to come to my house tomorrow night for our regular Friday budget session. Would he refuse to come? I really didn't know. He had never been angry at me before. But then, I had never bawled him out before either.

Friday afternoon, about 3:00 p.m., Lynn called.

"What time do you want us to come this evening?" she asked.

She sounded happy. And evidently Mike was coming.

"How about seven-thirty?"

I was waiting for them when they drove up in front of my house. Mike is never at a loss for words and I wondered what his opening line would be. He didn't disappoint me!

As I opened the door, he threw his arms out wide and said, "The prodigal has returned!"

"Oh, Mike, I'd never have forgiven myself if you hadn't."

He gave me a bear hug and then, with his arm around Lynn, we all headed for the dining room. Taking his seat, Mike said, "I sold the calculator to Lynn's mom—for $9.50. We really didn't need it, nor could we afford it. It was a good lesson."

Then, looking at Lynn, he added, "And I'm sorry."

"I'm sorry, too, Mike, for losing my cool yesterday. I really don't blame you for getting angry. But I'm glad it happened. It proves that we are both human. You have been so *good* about this whole business. No one would believe you were for real if you didn't blow your top, at least once, over having someone else hold the strings on your checkbook."

He shook his head. "I don't know why I was so determined. I guess I just wanted to spend some money on something besides bills."

"I do understand," I said, "but remember, I didn't give you all those bills. You did that all by yourselves. And besides, who promised you a rose garden?"

Lynn laughed and said, "Hey, if you do ever write a book about us, that would be a good title for one of the chapters."

No matter who you are:
    a young couple, like Mike and Lynn,
      a young single adult,
        a single parent,
          a not-so-young single,
      or an older couple,
gaining control of your "out-of-control" finances is no rose garden. Nor is it a picnic, nor even a barrel of fun! There will be times when, like Mike, you will want to throw self-discipline and caution to the wind and go out and buy something, *anything*. You may even be tempted to add a purchase to one of those past-due charge accounts. And you may not have a mate or a friend to remind you that you "can't afford it." In that moment, there is just you and your bright red budget book.

Please hang in there!

Before long you will see the light at the end of that

tunnel of debts. You will have learned how to plan, manage your income and spend wisely. Then you can go out and buy something—just for fun—and feel good about it!

Mike opened *his* bright red budget book. "We have to see how we are going to make the payment on our loan."

It would be six weeks before the first payment was due. Oil Company #1 would be eliminated by that time. It was going to be tight, but in just three short months the last of the seven charge accounts would be gone. After that, they might even be able to double up on the loan payments once in awhile.

Mike and Lynn were going to make it. Even this $3,000 loan didn't bother them. They knew how to face it and fit it into their budget. It wasn't a rose garden, but it was a lot better than that patch of unruly debts they started with earlier.

In the beginning of this book, I promised you a plan that was practical, exciting and fun. I hope you have found it to be true. I didn't, however, promise you a rose garden, either. The success of your financial recovery depends upon you. I know you can do it. Mike, Lynn and I pray that you will find some help and encouragement through their trials and triumphs and the story of their bright red budget book.

16/Now That You're Finally Out of Debt!

It would be impossible to end this book, having started you on the road to recovery, and not be concerned about your reaction when you are finally out of debt. There is a certain feeling of security in not having to make a lot of decisions regarding your money. For several months the only decision Mike and Lynn had to make was to stick to the budget. And stick they did—with a healthy determination.

The controls exercised by that bright red budget book were without mercy. Don't use even *one* credit card; don't buy *anything* beyond your meager allowances; don't write checks *after* payday, pay *every* entry in the payment schedule—and on and on.

But there comes a day when the need for those restrictions is lifted. You are free! You are finally out of debt. Now, you must begin making decisions. How are you going to use that available money? Your reaction could be one of several.

You could go beserk and start spending like mad; be afraid to spend any amount not listed in the bright red budget book; or, you could profit from past mistakes and exercise mature control over your future finances. And, of course, the latter is the reaction that I am hoping and praying you will have.

That bright red budget book was presented as a simple and fun way of gaining control of runaway debts, but *you* worked it. Your assets have been faithfully used to liquidate your liabilities according to the "Payment Schedule." The "Record of Progress" was included so that you might enjoy watching your debts decline and also to keep a visual account of your still-due balances before you. And the list of "Goals" was planned to give you something positive to think about—something to hope and plan for.

Now that you know how it is done, that same budget book, whatever its color might be, should remain as an effective and essential part of your family or personal finances. You still need a twice-monthly payment schedule to control your living expenses—a plan for staying within the bounds of your income. And instead of listing those past due charge accounts in your "Record of Progress," you can include the monthly amounts going into those two automatic savings accounts! Watching these grow is even more fun than watching declining balances on bad debts.

When Mike and Lynn first began to have a little money left over each payday, we discussed the necessity of learning to spend according to priorities. The subject came up one evening after Lynn said, "I need to get some new electric curlers, or have my old ones fixed."

Then, Mike cautiously added, "And we need to replace the broken valve on our inflatable spare tire before we have another flat."

You can only put off this type of spending for so long before it catches up with you. They had been going without everything except dire emergencies for months.

I said, "Why don't you go get them?"

Lynn smiled, "It's hard to realize that we do have the money—and I guess we're just a bit afraid to start spending again."

A small dose of this financial fear is good for the newly recovered budgeter! Your period of convalescence, however, need not be prolonged. The answer is learning to work with priorities. This is essential to good money management at any level. And it isn't nearly as limiting as it may sound.

We decided to add one more page to Mike and Lynn's budget book and title it, "Needs and Wants." These should not be confused with goals although they are closely related. A goal according to Mr. Webster is, "the end toward which effort is directed." Goals are usually connected with time and effort—like paying off bad debts or buying a house. Wants and needs fall into the category of "hair curlers" and "tire valves."

Once Mike and Lynn got started, their list began to grow. This is what the first one looked like:

NEEDS AND WANTS

NEEDS:
Hair curlers
Valve for tire
Slacks
Shoes for Bobby
Shoes for Mike
Shoes for Lynn
Tune-up for car
New tires

WANTS:
New swim suit for Lynn
Day at Glenwood Springs
New canister set
Sports jacket for Mike
New dress
New tennis racket

Listing "needs" first does not necessarily mean that all of these should be met before you can enjoy some of your "wants." Having a list, however, does let you weigh the importance of both needs and wants and determine your priorities. It helps eliminate buying on impulse. You can plan ahead and fit your spending into the most convenient payment schedule.

Mike and Lynn studied their list and decided to get the valve for the tire and the new swim suit—so they could drive up to Glenwood Springs and spend the day in the pool. Even I couldn't question that decision. They deserved it! I also have confidence that in the future that list of needs will get their vote nine times out of ten.

In case you are wondering if you will ever be out of debt and have the extra money to work on a priority list, let me show you what Mike and Lynn's payment schedule will look like when they finally pay off the last charge account and that dental loan.

The rent on the new apartment was $200 and has since been raised to $250. Their giving to the church has increased and the two automatic savings accounts are in operation.

PAYMENT SCHEDULE

1st	Tithe			60 00		
	Car payment			150 00		
	Savings #1			35 00		
	Groceries			100 00		
	Gasoline			40 00		
	Insurance			15 00		
	Utilities			35 00		
	Personal allowances			50 00		
15th	Tithe			60 00		
	Rent			250 00		
	Savings #2			35 00		
	Groceries			100 00		
	Gasoline			40 00		
	Telephone			9 00		
	Personal allowances			50 00		
	Take home pay			1200 00		
	Total expenses			1029 00		
	Balance			171 00		

151

When you are out of debt, take a good look at the schedule of payments used during your recovery period. Adjust them to cover all of your present monthly financial commitments. Add the amounts needed to relieve any pressure points. Now you are ready to enjoy a life where you are in control of your finances.

I hope and pray that you and your bright red budget book have become fast friends and that you will never be tempted to discard it in your debt-free world. Mike and Lynn join me in wishing you "happy finances for the future!"